The Writing Teacher's Handbook

JO PHENIX

Pembroke Publishers Limited

Other Books by Jo Phenix

*The Spelling Teacher's Book
of Lists*
*The Spelling Teacher's
Handbook*
Teaching the Skills
Teaching Writing

*Spelling Instruction That
Makes Sense* (with
Doreen Scott-Dunne)
Spelling for Parents (with
Doreen Scott-Dunne)

© 2002 Folens Limited

Pembroke Publishers
538 Hood Road
Markham, Ontario, Canada L3R 3K9
www.pembrokepublishers.com

Distributed in the U.S. by Stenhouse Publishers
477 Congress Street
Portland, ME 04101
www.stenhouse.com

This edition is adapted from a book written by Jo Phenix and first published by Folens Limited (UK).
E-mail: folens@folens.com

National Library of Canada Cataloguing in Publication Data

Phenix, Jo
    The writing teacher's handbook

ISBN 1-55138-142-7

    1. English language—Composition and exercises—Study and teaching (Elementary) I. Title.

LB1576.P482 2002   372.62'3   C2001-904112-8

Editors: Jennifer Steele, Karen Westall, Reina Zatylny
Layout artist: Suzanne Ward, Jay Tee Graphics
Illustrations: Debbie Riviere
Cover Design: John Zehethofer

Printed and bound in Canada
9 8 7 6 5 4 3 2 1

Contents

Introduction

Writing involves having something to say, and someone to say it to. Composition, and the need to communicate, form the heart and soul of the writing process, as well as the driving force to learning. To write successfully, we also need a wide range of vocabulary and syntax, and a knowledge of standard ways to get the message down in print.

Children come to school with a wealth of experience, knowledge and ideas, and they will add to this store daily. It will take many years of example, instruction, and practice for them to learn the skills and techniques involved in writing. It is probable that throughout their lives their ability to think and compose will outstrip their ability to record and communicate ideas in writing. An important goal for the classroom is to make sure children continue to generate ideas and language while they work through the long process of learning and refining their skills.

This book is about ways we can help children acquire and practice the skills they need to become writers. Our first task is to make writing a natural part of the daily activities of the classroom. Once children are writing freely and purposefully, then we can teach specific skills and techniques that will help them do the job better.

The ways we work with and respond to the children's writing will show them what we value, and thus what we want them to learn. We must not succumb to the belief that our role is to eradicate error wherever we find it. To be effective teachers, we must be more than proofreaders. We need to regard the children's writing not as tests of how well they perform, but as opportunities to help them refine their skills. The most productive kind of teaching reflects the nature of learning, and helps children move forward one step at a time.

Our purpose is not to produce writing; it is to produce writers.

"I wonder if the class does enough writing?"

Chapter 1

The writing environment

Providing the right environment

A writing environment involves two elements: the physical and the psychological. The rest of this book focuses on the latter; how to create a "writers' workshop" atmosphere in which children feel enthusiastic about writing, and free to learn new skills and take risks.

When you set up the physical arrangement of your room, you can consider two ways to organize for writing in the classroom:

✔ All the children can write at the same time during a designated writing period.
✔ You can set up a writing centre in which children can write at different times during the day.

The right conditions

Whichever system you choose to use, providing the following conditions can help children to be productive writers:

✔ **Privacy**. Children sometimes like to be alone. You can place bookcases, storage units, plants, or even a piano to make visual barriers. Working at a desk facing a divider gives more privacy than sitting across a table from other children.
✔ **Freedom from disturbance**. This does not necessarily mean silence. Children are usually less bothered by noise than we are, but they need to be able to work without interruption. Children are often more disturbed by movement than by talking. Visual barriers around areas of high activity can help children to concentrate on their tasks.
✔ **Space**. Sometimes children will need to spread out their papers, use reference materials, and use art materials to illustrate their work. Encourage the children to use the floor, the corridor, the library, or any space they need.
✔ **Equipment**. A variety of materials can encourage children to be more adventurous. Computers and typewriters can free children to focus on authoring skills, rather than secretarial skills.

Take the time to train children to work without disturbing one another, get the equipment they need, and know how to manage without you. This will free you to work with individuals or groups as the need arises.

Providing the right equipment

A writer needs paper
Different kinds of writing require different emphases. Using different media will help children to recognize when they need to scribble quickly, and when they need to attend to neatness and writing style. Different shapes and colours of paper can help to inspire more careful effort. Label your different kinds of paper, so that children know when to use them and for what purposes.

Note books
These are best for writing that will not go beyond a first draft, such as journals, notes, word lists, exploratory writing, and ongoing records. It is very difficult to add more material, rearrange paragraphs, or reword sentences in a book. For writing that children do in books, you can expect only editing for spelling and punctuation, and minor word changes.

You may find that children are unwilling to cross out and make changes in a book. Parents usually expect a book to be neat and tidy, and children therefore want this too. With a book, messy-looking writing stays with the writer for a long time. It is crucial that children know how to differentiate between when neatness matters and when making changes is more important.

First-draft paper
Loose paper is best for writing that will be revised and edited. Old, possibly already used, paper will encourage the children to focus on content rather than worrying about neatness. You could ask a local office or business to save waste computer and copying paper for you. The children could then do their first-draft writing on the backs of pages already used. This will also serve as a lesson in conservation.

If the children write on one side of the paper only, they can set all their pages side-by-side for revision. This will also enable them to cut and paste to rearrange paragraphs, and to insert new paragraphs and sentences.

Final-draft paper
Final-draft writing is intended for an audience; good-quality, final-draft paper supports this purpose. This should only be used when all revision and editing are complete, and the writing just needs to be recopied. At this stage, the children will focus completely on neat handwriting and attractive presentation.

Provide lined and unlined paper for the children to use for final drafts of stories, poems, reports and other writing that is intended for an audience. The quality of the paper will reinforce for the children that a final draft is something special, requiring extra care. To help children to write on unlined paper, provide sheets of lined paper they can slip underneath and hold in place with a paper-clip. You may need to trace over the lines with a black marker to make them show through.

Keep a box of folded book pages in different sizes. When they are ready to make a book, the children can select the right number of pages. You can keep a set of book covers ready to complete these books. (For more details, see Chapter 9.) You could also keep some sheets of school letterhead for writing letters to anyone outside the school.

A writer needs somewhere to store material

If the children are to use paper, they must be able to keep their work neat and tidy. They may have several pieces of writing on the go at the same time, and need to keep them separate.

Once a piece of writing is as complete as it is going to be, the children can staple the pages together. For larger pieces, such as long stories and reports, they can staple the pages inside a folded construction paper cover, and add a title to the front.

How to make a writing folder

You can give each child a file folder. However, while this is the simplest way of storing papers, it does not provide any means of separating or categorizing them. You could therefore staple or stick two or more file folders together to provide different sections. Label each section, for example, *Work in Progress*, *Finished Writing*, or *Tomorrow File*.

Alternatively, the children could make a three-section folder with construction paper or thin card by doing the following:

1. Cut a piece 70 cm (27 in.) wide by 40 cm (15 in.) high.
2. Fold into three 23 cm (9 in.) wide sections and open out again.
3. Fold up the bottom 8 cm (3 in.), and staple at the sides.
4. Cut an inverted V at each fold.
5. Fold the sides over the centre to make three sections.
6. Label each section.

Give each child half a dozen large paper-clips to clip onto the folder. These are then handy to keep papers sorted inside the folder.

Whichever way you choose, set up a file drawer or box with hanging files and label them alphabetically with the children's names. Teach the children to remove and replace their writing folder without disturbing the hanging files. In this way, the writing is always accessible for the child or for you.

The children can keep reference sheets either inside or stapled to the outside of their folder. For example, *Things I Can Proofread For*, *Editing Checklist*, *Stories I Have Written*. They can keep a list of theme words or specialized subject words as a reference.

A writer needs tools

Different writing implements will encourage children to experiment with sizes, styles and formats:

✔ Ballpoint pens	✔ Pencils with different hardnesses
✔ Felt-tip pens	✔ Calligraphy pens
✔ Coloured pencils	✔ Crayons
✔ Fountain pens	

Although pencils become a valuable commodity in a classroom, it is worth keeping some specially sharpened pencils available for final-draft work. Many children will also be encouraged to take greater care if they are allowed to use their own special pen.

The right tools will help the children to keep their writing neat and organized:

✔ Stapler	✔ File folders
✔ Paperclips	✔ Elastic bands
✔ Glue sticks	✔ Scissors
✔ Needle and thread	✔ Liquid paper
✔ Hole punch	✔ Sticky tape (double-sided)
✔ Erasers	✔ Self-stick notepads

Draw outlines on shelf mats to help children put tools away in the right place. One glance at the mat will show what is missing.

A writer needs a reference library

Keep a varied set of books that the children can go to for writing help:

✔ Dictionaries
✔ Thesaurus
✔ Atlas

Keep word lists you have built with the children. Put them in a ring-binder, or keep them on file cards:

✔ High-frequency words	✔ Spelling patterns
✔ Theme words	✔ Names
✔ Frequently misspelled words	✔ Addresses
✔ Subject-specific words	

Add some templates as models for the children to use:

✔ Letter with a heading	✔ Title page
✔ Addressed envelope	✔ Timetable
✔ Table of contents	

When you teach a lesson in a particular format, add its template to the collection. Keep them in a box, in a file, or punch them for a file folder.

Making recordings

It may also be useful to have a tape recorder with a microphone set up close to the writing area for children to make "oral" notes before writing. Children who make regular use of this facility might have their own cassette on which to store drafts for writing. This may be particularly useful for children who find it difficult to put their thoughts directly onto paper.

Why should we write?

A writer needs a reason to write

Any piece of writing constitutes a record of the ideas, thoughts and skills within our brains at any one time. Whereas an idea expressed through speech is lost and perhaps forgotten the moment it is uttered, writing is concrete and remains accessible to be polished and improved. From the time that we are very young, the urge to make such a permanent mark exists in all of us. Somewhere in the recesses of our minds, we need a reason to write, and an audience to appreciate our attempts.

Linking purpose to audience

Most writing falls into three main categories – expressive or personal writing, transactional or informative writing, and poetic or literary writing. Although we need to keep in mind the balance between these three types of writing in classroom activities, in practice the categories are best defined by the purpose to which the piece of writing will be put and its intended audience. These two factors will affect not only the need for presentational skills and clarity, but may well dictate the language features, style and formality of the text. For example, a keen birdwatcher might make a set of notes of personal observations of birds seen. If these notes are to be used as part of an explanatory text about the habitat or lifestyle of different birds, they cease to be purely expressive and become part of an informative work. At this point they become subject to the conventions of this type of text and their language style may need to be altered. Beginning from the purpose of the text in this way can help children understand the importance of different modes of writing.

Linking focus to purpose

Purpose	Important	Less important
Record information for personal use	Accuracy of facts, organization	Grammar, style, spelling, handwriting, neatness
Communicate a message to someone else	Accuracy of facts, clearness of expression, handwriting, spelling	Style, imagination
Create a work of literature to be published for others to read	Composition, style, organization, grammar, spelling, attractive presentation	
Persuade or convince someone	Ideas, style, organization, grammar, vocabulary, spelling, presentation	
Think through ideas	Variety of ideas, facts, creativity	Organization, style, vocabulary, grammar, spelling, neatness
Notes for writing a report	Accuracy of facts, brevity, organization	Composition, style, grammar, spelling, neatness
Speech	Accuracy, style, grammar, vocabulary, organization	Spelling, handwriting, neatness

Purpose and audience

The children should ask themselves two questions whenever they start a piece of writing:

✔ Question 1: What is it for?
✔ Question 2: Who is it for?

What is it for?　　Why is the writing being done and what will happen to it? The purpose will dictate what is important to focus on and what is not.

Who is it for?　　As teachers of writing, we should see ourselves as helpful editors, not as the only final audience.

Writing for oneself　　Writing intended only for the writer's own eyes does not need to be neatly written, correctly spelled and in complete sentences; these are at the discretion of the writer. In fact, attending to these is often a waste of time, and can distract the writer from the real purpose of the writing.

Writing in this category might include a diary, research notes, a memo, timetable, or shopping list. It is unlikely that any revision, editing, or recopying will take place.

Does the writing fulfill its purpose?

The most important aspect of writing for oneself is whether it fulfills its purpose for the writer. For beginning writers, this might mean can the writer read it again? For more experienced writers, it might mean is the information accessible and understandable when it is needed again?

Writing for a family member or close friend

We can often take a lot for granted when we write for a family member or someone we know very well. When we share many experiences, writing does not need extensive detail and explanation. Usually this is not a highly critical audience, and the writing is informal and quickly done. It will need a little more care than writing for oneself, but it would not typically go through extensive revision and recopying. This kind of writing might include personal anecdotes, postcards, letters, telephone messages, invitations, and greetings cards.

Writing for classmates and peers

These can often provide a critical but sympathetic audience for initial attempts. The first audience for a piece of work will often be a writing partner. Some classes have a weekly "Writers' Circle" (see p. 62) where children can opt to share their work with other children.

Writing for an unknown audience

When we do not know who our audience is, or when we are writing to a person we want to impress, then we usually take great care to make the writing correct, complete, well expressed, correctly spelled, and looking its best. We know that people will form an opinion of us based on how our writing looks and the content it contains. This kind of writing will go through the most revision and editing, and we will want the final presentation to make a good impression. This kind of writing includes books, articles, letters to the newspaper, job applications, advertisements, posters, instructions, and brochures. Appendix 1 (see p. 76) links the main purposes for writing to their main types, and lists their important features.

Setting specific writing tasks

Before the children set out to do a piece of writing, take some time to talk with them about the two questions discussed above, and give them some idea about the steps the writing will go through. Understanding this will help them learn what to focus on. Trying to attend to details that are not immediately relevant will distract children from what is important.

There are opportunities for writing tasks in every subject across the curriculum. Linking writing to particular subjects and topics can help children to see real purpose for the writing, as well as giving you the opportunity to teach the skills involved in the different formats or text types.

You can teach skills specific to different subject areas during your language instruction period. The writing you assign throughout the day in different subject areas will allow the children to practice these skills in the context of writing for real purposes. As you teach skills lessons, it can be helpful to keep a list of the features of different types of writing. You can display this list in the writing area, or give each child a copy for their writing folder. These features are not rigid sets of rules, but the children can use them as guidelines as they learn to use different styles and formats.

Key aspects of fiction and non-fiction formats

FICTION
- ✔ Plot
- ✔ Narrative structure
- ✔ Point of view
- ✔ Setting
- ✔ Character
- ✔ Use of dialogue
- ✔ Themes and genres
- ✔ Language

POETRY
- ✔ Forms and structures
- ✔ Rhyme and other sound patterns
- ✔ Rhythm
- ✔ Language

PLAYSCRIPT
- ✔ Setting
- ✔ Action
- ✔ Characters
- ✔ Dialogue
- ✔ Tension – tragedy/comedy
- ✔ Climax

NEWSPAPER REPORT
- ✔ Paragraph 1: Who? What? – main information
- ✔ Paragraph 2: Who? What? Where? When? Why? – elaboration on headline
- ✔ Paragraph 3: How? – further information
- ✔ Final paragraph: Less important details/lighter note/and finally (likely to be cut if space is tight)

Chapter

3

Organizing the time for writing

Keeping a balance between fictional and non-fictional writing

Traditionally, early writing development focused on fiction. There is a strong argument, however, for using much more non-fiction or informative writing from the outset. The clarity of purpose of a shopping list, the value of captions and labels, the relevance of a telephone message all relate to the world around us, and often require logical and sequential thinking. These should form part of early writing as the skills and strategies of the story form are being taught simultaneously.

You may wish to use the whole class, or shared sessions of a Literacy lesson, to teach the basic skills and strategies of writing, but the children will need immediate opportunities to apply those skills and strategies in different activities in subjects other than English.

Many topics and themes lend themselves either to fictional or non-fictional writing.

In recent years, the balance between fictional and non-fictional writing in the classroom has altered, requiring children to be much more flexible in their ability to organize what are often called "non-chronological" or informative types of writing. This means that rather than relying on the set "writing period", you need to plan, in advance, opportunities to study and develop different kinds and types of writing in the context of activities and tasks related to the whole curriculum.

The Literacy lesson still plays a central role in a whole curriculum approach to the children's development as writers, but planning for these lessons needs to begin when you make your long-term plans for the curriculum as a whole.

It makes much more sense for children to learn the skills and features of a particular type of writing in the context of tasks which have a real purpose. One kindergarten, for example, began by asking the children to "sign in" each morning. Many of them could only make their "personal mark", but this procedure served to emphasize that writing has a real purpose: that of recording those present each day.

Planning a scheme of work

A scheme of work needs to take into account both long-term and short-term objectives. Long-term objectives relate to an entire unit of work or topic, while short-term objectives relate to individual lessons. When making long-term plans for a particular unit or topic, it can be helpful to list the possibilities for different written outcomes.

The following table lists the types of writing the children can do for an Explorers theme. Each of these types of writing is discussed more fully in Chapter 6, but the table shows the possibilities for each writing type.

Theme Title: Explorers

Expressive writing	Transactional writing	Poetic writing
Letter home from a sailor	Labeled map of sailing route	Description of landfall
Captain's diary	List of provisions for ship	Haiku poem on loneliness
e-mails between a cabin boy on ship and sister at home	Instructions: how to use an astrolabe	Poems on board: thinking of home
Memoir: An old sea captain looks back	Recruiting poster for sailors	Sensory poem on storm at sea
	Diagram of the ship	Story: Adventure on board
	Article for newspapers back home	Acrostic poem using explorers' names
	TV news report on progress of the journey	Editorial: Why are we wasting tax-payers' money on exploring new lands?
	List of questions for a research project	

Once you have outlined a list of possibilities, you may then select those tasks which will be completed by every child in the class. These may require a whole class or shared delivery. Other tasks may then be differentiated as group-guided tasks or individual activities.

You may also decide which activities are best completed during the Literacy lesson, and which might be taught within a different subject period.

For fictional writing, an "ideas board" provides a similar planning aid for you and the children working on a specific story, novel, or poem.

The writing lesson

There are three main avenues for helping children to improve their writing:

✔ Teaching lessons before they write.
✔ Helping them individually while they write.
✔ Responding to their work after they write.

In the classroom, we can work for a balance of these three. Each will have its own particular areas of focus.

Whole class shared sessions	Guided group or individual support	Responding to writing
Motivating	Choosing topics	Providing feedback
Modelling	Developing ideas	Listening
Instructing	Organizing information	Evaluating
Patterning	Proofreading	Setting goals
Grammar	Sentence structure	
Spelling	Spelling	
Vocabulary	Vocabulary	
Presentation	Presentation	

There will be considerable overlap between whole class and group guided sessions, but the emphasis in the first should be demonstration and the modelling of good strategies. With a guided group, the focus will alter to provide support for children to attempt these strategies for themselves.

A balanced writing lesson may be organized as a four-step process:

✔ Inspiration – initiate the writing.
✔ Demonstration – whole class or group instruction.
✔ Experimentation – the children try out their own writing.
✔ Presentation – sharing time for audience feedback.

A dedicated Literacy lesson will allow you to organize differing levels of support. Whole class activities might be introduced and worked on through the whole class shared and whole class feedback sections of the lesson. One or two groups each day may be the focus of your or another adult's guided work. Other children may work independently in the writing area, knowing that their time for focused support will come later in the week. Tasks introduced through the whole class sessions might also be worked on in time designated for other subjects. Using the Explorers example on p. 15, children might carry out research for their maps and list of provisions as part of their History lesson.

Differentiating writing activities across groups and through different parts of the day in this way also encourages children to see writing as a total process in which the parts are often as important as the finished product, if not indeed more so. Many of the tasks they undertake may only reflect one or two steps in the writing process, but it is important that children understand how the whole process works.

This table illustrates one possible organization in which children receive instruction and feedback in different stages of the writing process. This is a guide to the kind of sequence you might use; regard it as a way of using your time productively, rather than a timetable to be strictly adhered to. Writing often needs more or less time to reach final draft.

	Whole class	**Small groups**	**Independent work**
Day 1	Initiate the writing: focus on purpose and audience. Text-level instruction: focus on subject matter/genre.	Children work in small groups to list ideas.	Children begin first draft. Individual conferences with teacher.
Day 2	Review of topic: model the writing. Sentence-level instruction: aspect of grammar/style.		Children continue drafts. Individual conferences.
Day 3	Text-level instruction: organizing information. Sequencing/paragraphing.	Peer group conferences. Share work to date, and make suggestions.	Children continue drafts. Individual conferences.
Day 4	Word-level instruction: vocabulary/spelling.	Children work in pairs to proofread and edit.	Children continue drafts. Individual conferences.
Day 5	Presentation instruction: focus on format/ handwriting.		Children prepare final draft. Individual conferences.

Follow up this writing project by providing opportunities for children to share their writing with the intended audience. For more information about text-level, sentence-level and word-level skills, see p. 67.

Teaching Grammar

Grammar is all about using words to construct sentences. Its purpose is to enable us to assemble language using established patterns of word order and function.

Learning about grammar is not a matter of taking apart other people's sentences, and putting names on the component parts. Grammar is a task of building, not one of demolition. The best way for children to learn grammar is to become familiar with the patterns of language, and to use them to put their own sentences together.

Any child who can talk already knows most of the grammatical patterns of language. In school, we can help children refine this knowledge, and expand the ways they can use language. We do not need to rely solely on specific lessons and exercises in grammar. Rather, we can help children use grammatical structures in order to write. They will be doing this as they use the patterning techniques described in Chapter 6.

It can be useful for children to know the terminology of grammar. If they do not know what things are called, it is very difficult to talk about them. Just as they learned all their other vocabulary by repeatedly hearing and using words in context, the children need to hear and use grammar terms. Young children learn the technical terms "word" and "sentence" quickly, not because we teach lessons, give exercises, or define them, but because we use these words in context daily. When they understand the functions of words, the children can learn other grammar vocabulary in just the same way.

Parts of speech

There are two kinds of words the children will need to learn about:

✔ Content words, that convey meaning, such as nouns, verbs, adjectives, adverbs, and pronouns
✔ Function words, that join the others together, such as prepositions, conjunctions and interjections.

Nouns

Nouns are anything you can recognize with your senses, any things you can see, hear, taste, touch, or smell. Children could build collections of nouns based on sensory awareness:

✔ List the nouns in everyone's pockets.
✔ List the nouns you have eaten today.
✔ Stand on the playground and close your eyes. List the nouns you can hear.
✔ Set up a display of hobbies (or of anything else). Everything in the display will be a noun. List them.

✔ Feelings and emotions are also nouns. Note these in your reading, and keep an ongoing list you can use in your writing.
✔ Test for nouns by putting "a" or "the" before a word.

Adjectives

✔ Children can print appropriate adjectives on scraps of paper, and attach them to nouns around the room. Challenge them to add new adjectives. This will demonstrate how adjectives can be used to describe nouns.
✔ The children can write acrostics using adjectives. They could use any noun, common or proper, as the subject:

C   courageous
A   adventurous
B   bold
O   optimistic
T   talented

✔ Numbers and colours are also adjectives, and collective words like *some, few,* and *many.* Children can test for adjectives by adding a noun.

Verbs

✔ In their reading, the children can note strong and weak verbs. The children can suggest and list strong verbs to replace weak verbs. They can then try to use stronger verbs in their writing. For example:

— Weak verb: go
— Strong verbs: depart, leave, scamper, travel, disappear

Raising awareness about grammar

✔ The children can add suffixes to change parts of speech.

— add "ly" to adjectives to make adverbs
    wise/wisely,
    kind/kindly
— add "y" to nouns to make adjectives
    rain/rainy,
    smell/smelly
— add "ment" to verbs to make nouns
    require/requirement,
    advertise/advertisement

✔ Use grammar terms whenever you talk about words. "Let's look at the action verbs the author has used here." "You use the adjective 'nice' a lot. Can you try and find more expressive adjectives to use?"
✔ The children can build word lists according to parts of speech. The lists on the next page follow a walk in the woods, with three groups listing different parts of speech.

Nouns in the woods	Tree adjectives	Animal verbs
tree	large	hop
bush	green	run
grass	leafy	hide
moss	tall	escape
birds	many	fly
branches	deciduous	slither
rabbits	coniferous	swim

Sentence structure

Sentence building

✔ Using words the children have collected as a resource, print individual words on cards, using a different colour for each part of speech you use. You could use one colour for function words. Children can use the cards to build sentences. They will have fun making crazy sentences.

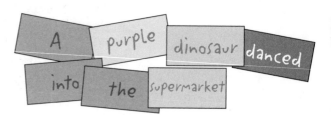

✔ Children can learn about phrases through poetry writing. When you build a sensory poem, like the one on page 59, ask the children to add a phrase saying where, when, or why.

✔ Challenge the children to find as many different words as they can that could start a phrase telling when or where. They can experiment with using these words to begin sentences. The result will be either a phrase (no verb) or a clause (including a verb). Even if the children do not know which is which, they will still be able to add more variety to their sentences.

Where	When
in	before
out	after
over	while
under	during
up	since
down	
through	
outside	

Sentence transformation

This involves substituting words in a sentence. It is one of the best ways to demonstrate for children the functions of different parts of speech.

✔ Start with a sentence, and print it in one line on the board. You can take the sentence from a shared-reading text, or create your own containing parts of speech to which you want to draw attention.

✔ Taking one word at a time, ask the children to suggest other words that could be used instead. They do not have to maintain the original meaning; it is not a search for synonyms. The test is whether they can read the word into the sentence, and still sound correct. List their suggestions below the word. Continue with other words in the sentence.

✔ Continue this with as many words in the sentence as you choose.

A a B b C c D d E e F f G g H h I i J j K k L l M m N n						
Lucy	climbed	fearlessly	through	the	old	wardrobe
Granny	wandered	wisely	in	an	alien	forest
Batman	gazed	eagerly	outside	a	monstrous	oven
I	galloped	shamelessly	around	a	green	satellite

By taking any word from each list, the children can make new sentences. Some may be nonsensical and funny, but all will follow the same sentence pattern.

Batman wandered shamelessly around the alien satellite.

If you use the pattern line-by-line, and make your substitutions horizontally, the children will use the same parts of speech to create new sentences. Each will follow exactly the same sentence pattern.

If you start out with a line from a poem, the children can create lines with exactly the same poetic quality.

It	was	a	dark and stormy night
Lancelot	was	a	deceitful and adulterous knight
Champlain	was	a	bold and fearless explorer

Teaching points

Transforming sentences will help children recognize the function of words. If they try to substitute words that are the wrong part of speech, they cannot read them into the original sentence.

✔ Each vertical list contains words in the same part of speech. By reading them vertically, the children will see and hear a word family. You can teach the terminology if instead of saying, "Give me a word" you say, "Give me another adverb that could go in here."

✔ Each verb in the list will be in the same tense. If you have 20 - 30 verbs in the list, the children will be able to see the most common verb tense endings, and also pick out irregular verbs.

✔ Similarly, the lists will illustrate common adjective and adverb endings. You can use these to point out the patterns for adding endings to words.

✔ If your original sentence contained a plural noun, you will have a list of plural nouns. The children will be able to pick out the most common plural endings, and also recognize irregular plurals.

Sentence combining

Joining short sentences to make one longer sentence will help children make their writing flow better and sound less disjointed. It will also teach them the function of conjunctions.

✔ As part of a shared-reading experience, draw the children's attention to simple sentences (The dog ran away.) and compound sentences (Although I called to him, the dog ran away.) The two parts should be separated by punctuation. The children can also note which part will stand alone, and which will not. You may not want to pursue this, but it does serve as an introduction to primary and subordinate clauses. If the children learn the concept now, they will more easily recognize the terminology later.

✔ With the children, start and keep adding to a list of words that can be used to join parts of sentences. If you want to teach the term "conjunction", you can help the children make the link with "junction" and "join".

A classroom list can include the following conjunctions:
because, although, and, but, either, until, as, unless, before, after, while

✔ When you read the children's writing, note to what extent they are able to use compound sentences. If you see mostly short, simple sentences, help the children link some of them with conjunctions.

✔ It is possible to write sentences that are too long and complex. If you see children using conjunctions too often, it may be a temporary stage as they experiment with a new idea. You could ask the children to read their sentences aloud, and to comment on the difficulty of following along.

Chapter
5

The writing process

Writing is not a single task, but rather a process involving four key stages:

✔ First draft
✔ Revision
✔ Editing
✔ Final draft

Each one of these stages has its own tasks, strategies, and skills. While many individual pieces of writing may not go through all of the stages, even the simplest writing tasks, such as writing a note to pass on a telephone message or putting a shopping list together, require a knowledge of the process.

"Hold the front page!"

Every piece of writing produced by the children will fit somewhere along the stages. Notes made from a reference book, for example, will fit into the *first draft* stage of the process and may go no further. An idea or draft for a story may be stored in a folder for some time before the writer decides to utilize it as part of a published piece and take it through the next two stages. Although the children may not consciously complete every stage of the process for each piece, they should be aware of what the full process involves.

Initiating writing

Through their Literacy lessons, children might collect personal anthologies of example texts to use when ideas run thin. As they read and study texts, children might also copy out and store examples of gripping story beginnings, effective endings or particularly apt descriptions, with appropriate references of course. (Assigning accurate information about references and sources at an early stage can save the writer a good deal of time later.) While children might be tempted in the early stages to plagiarize word by word, you can minimize this by altering the context or subject of the text.

Writing in the classroom is likely to fall into three main categories:

✔ Teacher-directed writing in the English lesson – assignments set by the teacher.
✔ Personal writing – topics chosen by the child.
✔ Writing arising from the subjects and topics of the broader curriculum.

Each of these is important to a classroom writing program.

Teacher-directed writing	✔ Make writing a part of every subject throughout the day. ✔ Make sure children have a wide experience of many different kinds of writing. ✔ Plan for many different audiences, both in school and outside. ✔ Structure writing in order to teach specific skills. For example, create an opportunity for letter writing, and teach the formats for headings, greetings, closings, addressing envelopes, and so on. ✔ Help the children to use writing as a way of exploring thoughts and ideas. ✔ Control the time spent on writing.
Personal writing	✔ Children can see how writing can play a part in exploring and pursuing their own interests. ✔ Writing on topics they are interested in and knowledgeable about can make writing easier. When children are confident about the content of the writing, they will be better able to focus on other aspects, such as genre and style, grammar and organization. ✔ Children can learn to make decisions about revision, editing and presentation. ✔ Personal writing is relatively risk-free, and the children can decide for themselves whether or not their writing is shared with others. ✔ Children can experiment and put into practice the skills they are learning in other parts of the writing program. ✔ We can foster self-motivation.
Writing arising from the subjects and themes of the curriculum	Just as children at school "learn to read to read to learn", writing across the curriculum subjects can take the same role. Children might learn through a Literacy lesson different ways of setting out information in the form of a chart or table. The first application of this knowledge, however, may come during a Math or Science lesson, which underlines the *purpose* for learning this strategy, and it will be through this subject that you are able to judge whether the child has mastered what has been learned.

First draft

Helping children to choose topics

Some children may have difficulty choosing their own topics, particularly if they are used to having all their writing assigned for them. If children claim they cannot think of anything to write about, do not be too ready to step in with a topic. Make suggestions, ask questions, direct them to sources of ideas, but leave the choices up to them. If this results in time spent doing nothing, don't worry unless the problem persists. Alternatively, suggest they have a brief chat with other children or read through some writing completed earlier by the children to give them ideas. Training the children to develop their own topics, styles, and motivation is worth the time lost. Reassure the children that every writer may experience writer's block at some time.

Ways to prompt writing ideas

✔ Many of the children's ideas will come from their reading or from television. Encourage them to make *brief* notes of episodes or action that they may wish to use later.

✔ Keep a file of pictures and photographs. These could come from newspapers or magazines. For example, in January you could ask the children to bring in old calendars, and ask a small group to choose interesting pictures for the file. If you mount the pictures on cards of the same size, laminate them and keep them in a file drawer or upright in a box, they will be easy for the children to take out and return. Alternatively, you could mount a picture inside a file folder, and put a blank page on the opposite side for the children to list interesting words associated with the picture.

When you have a collection, the children could categorize the contents, number them, colour-code them and insert dividers. You might have categories such as nature, people, animals, action, and weather. The children can browse through the pictures and choose one to stimulate writing. They might sometimes like to display a piece of writing along with the picture that inspired it.

✔ Keep an ongoing list of topics that the children have written about. These might give ideas, or spark similar interests.

✔ Provide opportunities for the children to share their personal writing with one another. They could do this by reading aloud in pairs or small groups, or publishing books for the classroom library. Having an audience is not only motivating for the writer, it can spark ideas for others (see pp. 61–65).

✔ Begin a list of story starters. You will get ideas from the children's reading and from their writing. Put each one on a file card, and keep it handy for any child who would like to browse for an idea. The children will be interested to see how different stories can come from the same idea. When several children have composed stories using the same starter, they could publish an anthology or slip them together into a file folder for others to read.

✔ You could also collect thought-provoking newspaper headlines, which could be pasted on cards and kept in the picture file. The children could choose a headline and create a story and illustration for it. Alternatively, you could make up some startling headlines to spark the children's imaginations.

Story starters and newspaper headlines

Story starters

✔ It was a dark and stormy night.

✔ There, on the beach, was an upturned boat.

✔ The old, elaborately carved box invited me to open it.

✔ The door stood ajar. Should I enter?

✔ It was the most exciting day of my life.

✔ One wave of the magic wand, and the deed was done.

✔ Ashok was the one who came up with the plan.

✔ That dog just would not behave.

✔ I knew when I invited Jane along on the picnic that it would be a disaster.

✔ Who would have guessed that a school trip could be so exciting?

✔ Janine stood poised on the edge of the diving board.

✔ The spaceship came to rest on a bare, rocky plain.

✔ "First, we must find a good name for our club," said Ricky.

✔ I only did it for a dare, but I never imagined what the result would be.

✔ "We're stranded on this island for at least a week," said Max.

Newspaper headlines

✔ Hot time in fireworks factory

✔ Local team brings home the gold

✔ Schoolgirl to the rescue

✔ Flying saucer sighted

✔ Teacher lost on school trip

✔ First news from Mars colony

✔ New invention makes schoolwork easier

✔ Each child can have a place to note down possible topics for future use. They might call this their "Tomorrow File". They could do this on the back page of a notebook, on a file card, or a page to keep in a pocket of a writing folder. From time to time, you could suggest an item for the tomorrow file, perhaps when the child tells you about something interesting, but it should be the child's choice whether or not it has possibilities.

✔ As children gain confidence similar ideas might be used for story-endings, which can prove even more of a challenge. Collecting good endings or beginnings from established authors may help children to think of new ideas.

✔ Suggest that the children go back through old pieces of writing, and find one they might like to add to or revise. Often looking through previous pieces will spark a new interest.

Situation cards

With the children's help, make a list of possible settings, characters and events. Print each word on a colour-coded card and bind each category with an elastic band. Children can pick a card at random from each pile, and create a story, newspaper article, poster, advertisement, script, or another genre of their choice around them. You can add other categories as you and the children wish.

Examples of settings, characters and events

Character	Place	Event	Time	Object	Word
monster	forest	race	past	violin	mysterious
robot	the moon	party	present	bucket	disaster
doctor	school	lesson	future	hat	conundrum
diver	tent	journey		computer	secretly
twins	beach	discovery		toaster	scientific
alien	bridge	sport		toboggan	purple
pilot	mountain	accident		sailing boat	incredible

All subject areas

Utilize "writing" sessions to initiate or complete work arising from other subjects. In a Literacy lesson, while other children are working in a guided group, some groups might research a topic raised during a Geography or History lesson. At other times you might use the guided group section to give direct support to children who are writing a set of instructions in Math or Science. Likewise, children might use a part of the day designated for History to apply in writing what they learned in their Literacy lesson shared section.

Preparing to write

Often, the hardest part of writing is getting started. How do we get the first sentence down on the page?

One factor that can help is to feel knowledgeable about the topic. This means knowing the right information, the right style, and the right words. It is often a good idea to encourage children to use personal expressive writing until they have learned enough of the skills of transactional and poetic writing to use specific formats and text styles (see Chapter 6). Build up a repertoire of ways for children to gain confidence before they begin to write.

Make a list

✔ What you already know about a topic.
✔ Questions you have about the topic.
✔ What you would like to include.
✔ What you think a reader might be interested in.
✔ Books you could go to for information.
✔ People you could ask for help.

Brainstorm

Brainstorming means writing down any idea that comes into your head that might be related to the topic. This is not the time to stop and analyze how relevant the ideas might be; that part comes later. The purpose of brainstorming is to generate a list of ideas from which to choose.

It is best to brainstorm in small groups with one person to record the ideas. If the children are too young to make notes quickly enough, you or a classroom volunteer could be the scribe. Recording with a marker pen on large paper will be helpful later when the group looks back at the list. Discourage the children from making value judgments or comments while the brainstorming is in progress because this discourages the free flow of ideas. You can help this by setting a time limit, perhaps three to five minutes. Later, children might keep their brainstorm notes in a folder to return to when they are stuck for ideas.

Talk with a partner

Put the children into pairs and ask them to share ideas. At first, you could start them off with some prompts related to the proposed topic.

✔ What would you need to know before starting to train a dog?
✔ What kinds of behavior can you train a dog for?
✔ What should every dog be trained to do?

With a little experience, the children will not need the prompts, and you can just ask them to work together and generate ideas.

Draw a picture

Children can often note down their ideas in pictures more easily than in words. We expect and encourage young children to draw before they write. It is a good idea not to eliminate this method of thinking too early. Children should be encouraged to see an illustrated sketch as the forerunner for making notes. Many adults doodle on paper as a way of focusing their thoughts. One of the benefits of collecting thoughts through art is that a picture does not have to be drawn sequentially – we can start with any aspect, adding to it as we think of more ideas or details. Children may be more used to the idea that a picture grows and changes than being able to recognize that writing may evolve in the same way. In the early stages, some children will find it helpful to make these pictorial "random thought notes" on separate slips of paper which can be moved around physically to achieve a satisfactory sequence.

Adapt familiar stories

By examining the structures of familiar stories, children can build up a skeleton or framework around which to build a "parallel plot". This technique may also help them to see that a simple plot structure can be used as the basis for an infinite variety of stories.

Do some research

Writing is most difficult when we feel we do not know enough about the subject, or when we feel we have nothing to say about it. Imagine a situation where you have a piece of information – a story, some gossip, a joke – that you just can't wait to tell someone. This kind of situation is also the optimum starting point for a piece of writing.

Research does not necessarily mean pouring over reference texts. It simply means finding out what you need to know. Develop a source list for your classroom:

How to find out

Where	Who	How
School library	Classmates	Personal contact
Public library	Teachers	Phone
Books at home	Parents	Fax
Newspapers	Neighbours	Email
Posters	Friends	Letter
Index	Experts	Interview
Table of contents		Photograph
Advertisements		
Telephone directory		
Local businesses		

You can also develop a list of expertise in your own classroom. Ask the children and any other people your children have contact with in school, such as office staff, cleaners and volunteers, to become part of a talent bank. These experts can give advice or information when needed.

Our talent bank

Subject	Expert
Stamp collecting	Robert
Care of horses	Angeleena
Camping	Mr. Westaway
Football	Joshua
Local history	Miss Worsnop
Building model airplanes	Rajiv
Breeding tropical fish	Mavis
Birdwatching	Mrs. Goldthorpe
Proofreading	Felicia

Make an outline

An outline is a list. Rather than a list of facts or details, it is a list of topics and headings that might be included in a piece of writing. It can be very helpful in directing and organizing the gathering of ideas and information, although it becomes a drawback if it places restrictions on the writing. It is most helpful if you see the outline as something that will be moulded and adapted as the writing progresses. If the finished product turns out to be nothing like the outline, this should not necessarily be seen as a problem, as the outline's purpose was to get the writing started.

An outline can be for a specific writing project. This will look a lot like a table of contents, and will be a list of points that should be included. The writer can then work on each one in turn. For example:

A visitor's guide to my city

✔ Historical attractions
- buildings
- historic sites

✔ Cultural activities
- theatre
- music
- art

✔ Sports
- to watch
- to play

✔ Useful information for tourists
- where to stay
- where to eat
- where to shop

✔ How to get there
- local map

An outline can also be more generic and represent a style or genre of writing. It can then become a model for many pieces of writing.

Mystery story

✔ Opening
- set the scene
- introduce the main characters

✔ Discover the problem
- anecdote

✔ Add to the problem
- series of anecdotes

✔ Solve the problem
- ending

An outline can also form a checklist at the revision stage of writing, to make sure that nothing has been omitted.

Writing frames

A writing frame is a model of a specific writing format. You will find examples of poetic writing frames under Patterning Techniques later in Chapter 6. A frame might be a series of headings, such as those found in a recipe: Name of dish, Illustration, List of ingredients, Instructions. Think of this as a "fill in the blanks" kind of frame, where children write the appropriate information under each heading. Another example might be "How to address an envelope" and this could be a sample to be used as a model. When you have introduced the children to a particular format, leave a frame or model in the writing area for the children to use as they need it.

Dressing up

Acting out a situation through dramatic play is one way in which young children make up stories. This can work well with older children too. Keep a few simple props in a box – hats, capes, magnifying glass, walking stick, tools, dolls, puppets, toys – and encourage the children to create a scenario or story. If two children work together in this way, and then write a story together, they can continue their play-acting throughout the creative process. This is also a good stimulus for writing dialogues and scripts.

Tell a story

Encourage the children to use props such as a puppet, doll or model to tell a story orally. Children will be used to hearing stories read aloud, and will recognize that stories often have their own special conventions. The words 'Once upon a time ...' can set a mood rooted in oral tradition and help children to activate ideas and language learned from reading and listening to literature. A puppet is an uncritical, non-threatening audience, and can allow children to work out their ideas prior to writing.

Use a tape recorder

Some children may be more able to verbalize their first thoughts and ideas than to write them down. Make a tape recorder available so that the children can talk through their ideas, either alone or with a partner. They can then listen and select ideas they will use. This could lead to brief note-making.

A tape recorder can also be a valuable way to break the cycle of monotonous "news". Provide an opportunity for children to recount a visit, birthday treat or weekend events onto tape, allow them to listen with some writing partners and discuss how this might be shaped into an account. Encourage the children to discuss their favourite occupations on the tape, such as karate lessons, gardening, swimming, computer games or mountain biking. For example, Michael, who was not the keenest of writers, was revealed by his oral account to be an expert gardener with a wealth of knowledge about growing flowers, herbs, and vegetables.

These oral accounts can often reveal much more interesting and absorbing details than would emerge in the children's written "news". What is more, they are likely through their spoken account to use vocabulary that they might avoid in their writing. Their partners can then work to help them to transcribe and shape the written piece.

You can link the use of a tape recorder with drawing. Ask the children first to draw a series of pictures, then record what they will write to go with each picture. This could be a narrative or information for a report. They can then transcribe their own words from tape to print. This often results in longer pieces of writing, as the composing is done without the constraints of handwriting speed and spelling, which often slow down a child's creative thinking. This is an ideal way to put the drafting process into action, as the children can concentrate on one aspect at a time: first generate the ideas, then formulate the language, and finally write the words down.

Start in the middle

An opening sentence is often the hardest to write. It is also one of the most important sentences of a piece of writing. Some children write and cross out constantly as they struggle to make just the right beginning. Suggest they leave this opening sentence until last. Even an opening paragraph is often best written when the main body of the writing is complete.

Similarly, the title can be a stumbling block. A title is often a summary of what the piece is about, and can best be created when the writing is finished. Encourage the children to leave a space for the title, or pencil in a "working title" which can be changed later if necessary.

Writing the first draft

First-draft writing is the first attempt to get thoughts down in words. It can take different forms, depending on the style of the writer. Some writers like to think ideas through first, formulate language in their head, then write a coherent and organized product. Others write in a fashion that is often disorganized and incomplete. Yet others write in sentence fragments, odd words and phrases, notes to oneself. All of these are acceptable ways to make a first draft.

The most important thing for children to learn about a first draft is that it is not intended to be a finished product to share with others or to be evaluated as their best work. It is the raw material with which the writer will work, there to be moulded into a final, polished form. It is rarely possible for writing to turn out in its best form in one attempt. There are so many different skills involved in writing that it is far more productive to focus on them one at a time. There is an order in which to accomplish everything necessary to producing a finished piece of writing; it does not all have to be done at the same time.

Some pieces of writing never go beyond the first-draft stage. The degree of revision and editing is a factor of purpose and audience. Some writing is never intended to be anything more than a first draft; for example, memos, diaries, personal letters, records, lists, research, and notes.

The first draft is often the hardest aspect of tackling a writing task, as it is here that the writer develops ideas and language. It is usually easier to change and improve a piece of writing than to create the draft in the first place. Fear of what it might turn out like, as well as fear of spelling mistakes, can deter children from getting started. Viewing the first attempt as a draft can free children to take risks.

Carving in stone

One reason the opening of a piece is so difficult is the belief that whatever is written is the final product. Children who are afraid of making mistakes often grow into reluctant writers. This is the tyranny and the limitation of single-draft writing. Remind the children that they are not carving in stone. Anything they write can be changed later. When children are familiar with using the drafting process, they will feel more comfortable with writing the easy parts first, and adding and rearranging sentences and paragraphs later.

Teaching first-draft writing

✔ Teach the children to print "First Draft" at the top of their paper before starting to write. This is their license to take risks, to make mistakes, to cross out, and to look messy. It is their "get out of jail free" card. Show them that in any writing labeled "first draft" they are expected to focus on content, and only their ideas and effort will be evaluated.

✔ Model the creative process when you write on the board. Make rough notes. Do not attempt to make your handwriting neat and orderly. Talk through your own thinking process; for example, "I'm not sure of the spelling of that word. I'll mark it to check later." Cross out, rather than erase. Use arrows to insert new words and sentences.

✔ Use an overhead projector as a way to model first-draft writing. When you are asking the children for words and ideas, jot them down quickly while the children watch. You can go over them afterwards to select, prioritize, eliminate, and change them. You can then make a second, more organized draft as the children watch.

✔ When you read or respond to the children's first-draft writing, make sure you comment only on the content. This must be the focus of a first draft. If you mention such things as paragraphs, grammar, spelling and neatness, even to praise, you will be sending a message that these are important features of a first draft. In fact, they belong at later stages of the writing process and can impede the writing of a first draft.

✔ Use the term "first draft" rather than such expressions as "rough copy". Using the correct writing terminology can help children to think like writers. Even writing that will only ever be a first draft can still be called a "draft". The most threatening and inhibiting aspect of writing is what others might think of you when they read it. Seeing a draft as temporary and private can help children to become more confident in their writing. There will be later opportunities to focus on making a good impression.

✔ Give children opportunities to write using a *computer*. The computer is a perfect composing machine, as it makes adding, deleting and changing so easy. There can be no risk in writing on screen, as anything can be changed before the copy is printed. Once children learn the concept of drafting on a computer, they will be more ready to transfer these skills to all their writing.

✔ Do not give marks or grades for first-draft writing. A good writer is not someone who gets everything perfect in one draft. Evaluate only the child's ability to make a reasonable start. Qualitative assessment should be of the final draft, when the child has had every opportunity for revision, editing and neat presentation. For your own private information, you may wish to make notes about a child's spelling, handwriting and first-draft style. This can be useful and will tell you what comes automatically for the child. It will not give you reliable information about a child's spelling knowledge, handwriting skill, ability to organize information, and so on that can be achieved in a considered and edited final draft.

Revision

Revision differs from editing in that it focuses on content, style, grammar, vocabulary and organization, rather than on spelling, punctuation, handwriting and other surface features. Revision involves reading your writing with a critical eye and deciding how you can make it better. To revise, you must put yourself in the position of a reader, and see your writing from the outside.

Revision and editing

If you separate the two aspects of revision and editing by using different terms for them, you can help children to understand what they are to focus on during each operation, and which should come first. It is not productive to spend a lot of time on proofreading and editing until revision is complete; why make corrections in a sentence that might be changed or even disappear altogether?

Through their reading, children can begin to pinpoint and learn the features of the main types of informative texts, noting the structure to use when organizing their own work of a similar type.

Getting the content complete

You can help children to work on content by developing a list of questions they can ask themselves as they reread their writing. Even beginning writers can do this, but the number of questions they can consider will increase as they become older and more experienced.

Questions to ask about content

✔ What did I set out to write about?
✔ Have I included everything I need to say?
✔ Who will be reading this?
✔ What questions might the reader still need answers to?
✔ Is there anything irrelevant that I should take out?

It is often helpful for children to get some feedback at this stage. You or another child can read the writing, or listen as the author reads it aloud, and make suggestions for revision. When the children first work in pairs or small groups to help with revision, you could guide their thinking by giving them one or two suggestions and guidelines to follow.

Guidelines for peer-group feedback

For beginners:

✔ Say one thing you liked about the writing.
✔ Ask one question to find out more.

For older children:

✔ Say which part you liked best and explain why.
✔ Point out one part that needs to be improved. Say why.
✔ Give one idea to make the writing better.

Organization

Organizing a piece of writing may involve sequencing and paragraphing.

Sequencing

Sequencing is particularly important when writing instructions and directions. The sequencing of activities is also a first step to understanding paragraphing.

Ways for children to practice sequencing

✔ Retell a personal anecdote, either orally or in writing.

✔ Relate a personal experience, such as a journey.

✔ Ask very young children to draw several *pictures* to tell a story, rather than just one. They can number their pictures to emphasize that the order is important.

✔ Cut up the frames of a comic strip and ask the children to reassemble them.

✔ Follow step-by-step instructions; for example, a recipe.

✔ Write directions for someone to get from your house to school.

✔ Make a timetable of your complete day, from waking to sleeping.

✔ Teach someone a card game.

✔ List several local attractions, locate them on a local map, plan an itinerary to visit them all, then write a tourist guide.

Paragraphing

Paragraphing means categorizing information, or putting together points and ideas that belong together. It is the same skill that children use when they sort buttons by colour, or plants by genus, or when they hang their clothes on their own peg. Any child who can put items away in the right desk, bag, or cupboard understands the skill of paragraphing.

In writing, it is more difficult initially because sentences on a page do not look different from one another as buttons do. When we paragraph, we sort something that is invisible, namely ideas and meanings. We can make paragraphing easier by restoring some of the visual aspects that children are used to.

The best tools for paragraphing are scissors, and glue or tape. Just as children sort objects by putting them into separate piles or containers, they can sort ideas by cutting apart their sentences, and putting them into piles according to their content. Each pile can then be sequenced to build a paragraph.

Ways to teach paragraphing

✔ Cut apart the individual frames of three different comic strips and ask the children to reassemble them. To do this, they will need to categorize according to the comic strip, then sequence each frame. This is exactly what they need to do with sentences in their own writing.

✔ Cut apart the sentences of an article of two or three paragraphs and ask the children to reassemble the sentences into the original number of paragraphs. At first, you could give a title to each paragraph, to act as a category name.

An essential tool for any writer.

✔ Any categorizing or classifying activity in any subject area will reinforce the concept of putting together what belongs together. When the children sort in Math or Science, draw their attention to the similarity with paragraphing.

✔ In the children's reading, draw their attention to the paragraphs and talk about the content. Ask the children to summarize a paragraph in one sentence. This makes an excellent small-group activity, as the children will need to talk about the topic of the paragraph in order to summarize. This can help children to recognize that a paragraph has unity of meaning.

✔ Study the content of paragraphs in *newspaper reports*. Because editors cut news reports from the end to fit the available space, writers put as much information as possible, written very briefly, into the first paragraph, and add supporting detail in successive paragraphs. This will help children to see that paragraphs serve different functions. It may also help them to learn that you can read a newspaper very quickly and get a synopsis of the news by reading only the first paragraph of each article.

✔ Often, the first sentence of a paragraph states what topic the paragraph is about. This is called a "topic sentence". All the other sentences in the paragraph will support and add to the statement in the topic sentence. You can give the children a framework for writing a report by providing them with several topic sentences, and asking them to add two or three sentences of detail to complete each paragraph. For example:

- Monkeys make their homes in the high canopy of the rainforest.
- Monkeys eat food from many different plants.
- Monkeys live in close family groups.
- Some monkey species are endangered.

✔ It is very hard to cut and paste sentences in a book. You will find it easier to help children to rearrange their writing into paragraphs if they write on one side of loose sheets of paper. As they will be working with first-draft writing, this does not need to be high-quality paper. The choice to start on paper rather than in a notebook will depend on whether the children expect to revise and edit, which will in turn depend on the purpose of the writing and the intended audience, if any.

✔ Talk through paragraphing as you work with children on their writing. Say, for example, "You are starting a new topic here; better start a new paragraph." You can do this same kind of modelling as you write on the board while the children watch. "That paragraph was all about _____. Now we'll start a new paragraph on _____."

✔ In their reading, draw the children's attention to the way paragraphs are separated. Sometimes they are indented and sometimes there is a blank line between them. The choice of which to use is largely personal, but handwritten letters to friends and family tend to be indented, while business communications leave a blank line.

✔ Use the term "paragraph" many times throughout the day. The more often you use the term, and the more you talk about paragraphs, their purpose and their content, the more the children will understand them and use them in their own writing.

✔ Once the order of paragraphs has been settled it is often useful for children to read through their work to check that the language style is cohesive. Paragraphs may have been composed at different times, using different sources of reference, and the revision stage is a good time to check that if the present tense has been used for a report, for example, any change of tense is deliberate.

Vocabulary

Once the content is complete and organized, the children can look at the individual words they have used, and see if they can improve on them. You can direct them to one particular aspect of vocabulary, or give them a checklist to follow for themselves.

Look for
overworked verbs

✔ Verbs such as *did, went* and *said* can often be replaced with stronger, more expressive verbs. Work with the children to develop a list of such overworked verbs, add to them as you notice others, and suggest that the children try to avoid them.

✔ Collect alternatives for overworked verbs and keep the lists handy. The children can refer to the lists as their own personal thesaurus when they are revising their writing.

── Words for "said" ──

cried	echoed	replied
responded	shouted	called
whispered	asserted	uttered
explained	suggested	commented
asked	warned	urged
described	announced	stated
inquired	answered	yelled
expostulated	riposted	snapped

Look at adjectives

✔ Teach the children the function of *adjectives* and draw their attention to them in their reading.

✔ Make adjectives a particular focus for a week. Talk about adjectives that the children find in their reading. Invite them to select passages that use adjectives well, and share them with the rest of the class. They can then select passages from their own writing to show how they use adjectives.

✔ Once in a while, ask the children to underline each adjective that they have used in a story or piece of descriptive writing. They can then assess whether they have used enough (or too many), whether they have used overworked adjectives, and whether they can add or improve on any.

✔ Start a list of interesting and expressive adjectives. Encourage the children to add to it whenever they come across one they like, or feel they would like to have for future reference. As a short exercise, you can choose an adjective of the day from the list, and put it on the board. Ask the children when they have a spare moment during the day to write a sentence using that adjective, and put it in a box. At the end of the day, choose several of the sentences to read aloud.

✔ Use the term "adjective" daily. The best way for children to learn new terminology is to use the words in context.

✔ You may find that when you draw children's attention to adjectives they start to overuse them, attaching several to every noun. Don't worry about this; it is an experimental stage that will sort itself out. It may take children a while to find a happy medium when using adjectives.

Check technical words

When the children are writing on theme topics or producing factual reports, they may need to use technical language associated with the subject. They will find it useful to have a list of terms they might need for that subject. When you are starting a new topic, generate a list of special words and add to it as the theme progresses. As the children edit, they can check that they have used the correct spellings and meanings.

One word of warning: make sure the children do not think that the words on such a list are to be memorized. It must not become a spelling list to prepare for a test. At the end of the topic or project, the class or group might decide from the list which words they may need in the future, and they can transfer these to personal spelling logs or reference lists. Spelling is best learned by collecting words into families and looking at the patterns, not by trying to memorize individual words. Many theme words will be too difficult for the children to remember; this is why a reference list is so useful.

Editing

Putting on your public face

Editing means putting on your best face for the public. You can explain this to the children through an analogy they will understand. It is rather like putting on your best clothes for special occasions, and cleaning the house when company is coming.

Audience awareness

The first step in teaching editing is to show children what it is for and why it is important. Making your writing as correct and attractive as possible is like combing your hair before having your photograph taken. There are times when we all want to look our best. Similarly, there are times when this is not productive. We do not put on our best clothes to work in the garden or polish the car. Nor do we get out our best notepaper to make the shopping list. Sometimes speed and convenience, as well as saving money and labour, are more important than looking neat and clean.

The same principles apply in writing. Purpose and audience will dictate the type and amount of editing we will need to do. The more we care about the kind of impression we make on our reader, the more effort we put into editing. Thinking that editing and recopying must always be done is as non-productive to writing as thinking it need never be done, and can reduce writing to being just a school subject, rather than a real-life activity. If a child has to ask whether spelling matters, the child does not understand the purpose of the writing, nor the place of editing.

*Demonstrating the
purpose of editing*

✔ Provide many opportunities for the children to write for different audiences: classmates, parents, other classrooms, people outside school and family. Then you can talk about the kind of impression they will want to make with their writing.

✔ Do not expect children to edit all their writing. Children can also learn the place of editing by seeing when it is not necessary.

✔ Give feedback on spelling, handwriting, and neatness before a piece of writing is to go public. This will reinforce its importance at this stage.

✔ Ask a publishing company or newspaper to provide examples of edited copy showing editorial markings. This will help children to see that editing is necessary for everyone, even adult, professional writers.

✔ Expect final-draft writing to be fully edited and as correct as it can reasonably be. Provide whatever help a child needs to accomplish this. If children write a final draft which still contains many spelling and punctuation mistakes, then it cannot be considered final, and should be redone before going on public view. This will help the children to see that editing before they start a final draft can save them a lot of time and trouble.

The Editor is IN!

✔ Offer your own services, or those of an adult volunteer, as editor. Post a sign to say when you are available and invite children to bring their writing to you for editing. As an editor engaged for the job, you can mark every error or omission, and help the child to make the necessary corrections.

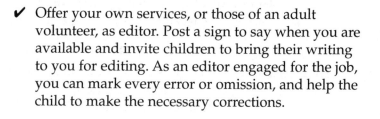

Editor as helper

As you edit the children's work, make sure that they realize that helping in the role of editor is very different from correcting in the role of examiner.

✔ Train a group of older children to be volunteer editorial assistants. You could establish a certain time when they visit your classroom, or set up lunchtime sessions. Children could make appointments to work with these assistants to edit their own writing. The older children would also gain some valuable practice in proofreading at the same time.

✔ Set up a classroom publishing operation (for more information, see Chapter 9). Accept nothing for publication that has not been fully edited, either by the child, or by someone else. For younger children, this will mean providing all the help they need for what they have not yet learned to do. There is no greater motivation for writing and editing than having a polished, published book to share with the world. Classroom support assistants, both paid and volunteer, can play a vital part in this role.

The editorial process

Editing involves two processes:

✔ Proofreading, or finding errors and omissions.
✔ Copy editing, which is making the necessary corrections.

Proofreading

Proofreading is not like most other kinds of reading. As we teach reading, we try to move children as quickly as possible beyond reading word by word to reading for larger units of meaning. The more fluent the reader, the less attention is paid to the individual words on the page. We know that in reading it is possible to skip over words and even whole phrases without detracting from the meaning. This is one reason why we read far more quickly when we read silently. When we proofread, however, it is important not only to look at all the words, but even to examine the parts of words. Thus proofreading has its own set of reading skills.

Strategies for teaching proofreading

✔ Proofreading is not a skill of looking "at" words; rather it is a skill of looking "for" particular aspects. If we know what we are looking for, we are more likely to find it. It is not usually effective to say to a child, "Read through your writing and see if you can find any mistakes." Often the child reads through and can find very little. When you ask a child to proofread, name some specific aspects to look for. For example, "People are talking on your page. Find what they are saying, and put quotation marks around it." Or, "Make sure you have a capital letter at the beginning and a period at the end of every sentence." If children are preparing a final draft, and need to proofread for everything, then they should look for one aspect at a time.

✔ Even professional editors do not expect to be able to check everything in one reading of a text. It is far more productive to look at one aspect at a time, for example sentences, punctuation or spelling. You can provide an editing checklist for each child. Children might also take it in turns to act as "Punctuation editor" or "Speech editor" or "Theme words editor", giving them practice in these areas. Children who have trouble finding their own mistakes may learn the skill of proofreading by looking at the work of others.

Writing checklist

Ask yourself these questions when you proofread your writing. You will not need to ask every question for every piece of writing. Choose the ones you think are important for that piece.

About my topic:
✔ Have I left out anything important?
✔ Do I have my ideas in the best order?
✔ Will my reader understand what I am saying?

About my style:
✔ Does my beginning interest the reader?
✔ Have I used interesting words?
✔ Do I have a good ending?

About spelling:
✔ Have I used words that can have more than one spelling?
✔ Have I chosen the correct spelling?
✔ Have I used the correct plural ending on plural words?
✔ Have I used apostrophes in contractions?

About punctuation:
✔ Are characters speaking? Have I used speech marks?
✔ Are there questions that need question marks?

About sentences:
✔ Have I used capital letters to begin sentences and names?
✔ Do all my sentences make sense?
✔ Have I left out any words?

Adapted from *Spell Check. A Spelling and Grammar Activity Book, Grades 4–6.* (Harcourt Canada 1998)

✔ Limit the task for beginners by putting a mark at the beginning of a line that contains an error. Ask the children to find a specific error in that line. For example, "Find the word you have left out." Or, "Find the missing capital letter."

✔ Suggest that the children place a ruler below each line as they are reading. This will help them to focus on a small amount of text at a time. It may also be helpful if the children point to each word as they read it, either with a finger or a pencil. This slows down the reading and makes sure that children look at each word individually.

✔ Often children can find omitted words and punctuation by reading their piece aloud. This does not need an audience. Teach the children that if the writing does not sound right, or if they have to reread a sentence to get it right, then something might be missing or misplaced.

✔ It is often easier to find someone else's mistakes than your own. When we read our own writing, we know what we are trying to say, and often focus on the intended meaning rather than what is actually written down. Put the children in pairs so that they can proofread for one another.

✔ It is more useful to sit beside a child and help with proofreading than to take the writing away and mark errors. First, you can model the process of proofreading while the child watches, at the same time discussing the errors that you have found. Editing in the child's absence has a connotation of fault-finding, and it is hard for children to see this as positive and constructive.

Copy editing

You can teach the concept of copy editing long before the children are able to do any for themselves. When you are putting up a sign, writing a letter, or scribing as the children dictate, do a first draft either on the board or on the overhead projector, or in any way that the children can watch. Then check the spelling, add punctuation, and plan the layout before making a final copy. This will not only show the children the process you go through, but reinforce the concept that editing helps to get the final product correct and looking nice.

✔ When the children have a story to share, a poem to display, a letter to send, an invitation to make, or a sign to put up, ask them to do a draft on scrap paper. Then when the content is complete, offer your help as editor. You can say such things as, "Let's see what you need before you do your final draft." Go through the writing with the child, and talk through the changes you are making: "This is a new sentence; you will need a capital letter here." "This is how you spell this word." In this way, you can correct all the errors and omissions, but in a constructive and helpful way, rather than in a critical manner.

✔ The overhead projector is an ideal tool for teaching editing skills. With the child's permission and removing the name, you can make a transparency of a child's writing, and use it to talk through the editing with the class or a group of children. You could follow the order of operations suggested in the Writing checklist (see p. 42), and ask the children's help in editing one aspect at a time.

✔ Use the term "editing" rather than "correcting". Correcting has an evaluative connotation, and children often see this as negative criticism.

✔ Expect children to edit for only those skills they have already learned. In the early stages of writing, all editing will need to be done by someone else, preferably while the child is present. As the children learn more about spelling, punctuation and so on, they can take on more responsibility themselves. The children can keep their own lists of aspects they can edit for, and add to them as they go along. This will also serve as a growing and visible list of what a child is learning, and can give confidence to both child and parent. You can make the children responsible for the points on their lists; do not accept a child's editing as finished until these are done.

43

To recopy or not to recopy?

Laborious recopying can discourage children from editing. The learning is in proofreading and making the necessary changes, rather than in recopying the writing. You might occasionally ask a child to edit for certain aspects as a learning exercise, but if there is to be no audience, recopying will serve no useful purpose. It will just make writing a boring and purposeless activity, and can result in children writing less.

Individual teaching through editing

It may seem too time-consuming to work on proofreading and editing with each child, rather than taking the writing away to be corrected. However, the potential for learning is so much greater that it is worth taking the time. When children get back their writing proofread by someone else, it is hard for them to see editing as a positive part of the writing process. Even when you write positive comments, what they will see first is everything they did wrong.

What makes personal teaching possible in the classroom is the realization that not all writing needs to be edited. Much of the writing the children do will not be intended for an audience. Choose which pieces you and the children will work on, and limit the amount to what you can reasonably accomplish. It is better to work productively on a few pieces of writing than to spend time on laborious correcting and marking that not only takes so much time, but also works against the constructive attitudes you are trying to promote.

Reading what the children write

It is a good rule of thumb that if you have time to read everything the children write, then they are not writing enough. The learning is in the children writing, not in us reading their writing. Concentrate on making the most of the teaching opportunities you do have.

Producing writers, not writing

The purpose of classroom writing is not that every piece of writing should come out looking perfect. Do not fall into the trap of thinking that we need to teach everything with every piece of writing. That will lead to information overload for the children, and very little real learning. It is enough if they learn one new skill, or practice one they already know, each time they write. Our ultimate goal is that children learn to think and work as writers. Once they can do this, they will know how to work towards writing that is correct.

Final draft

Writing a final draft

A final draft is the public face of writing, the one the reader will see. It involves such things as handwriting, page layout, format, size, illustration and choice of paper. Attractive presentation is a courtesy we pay to our readers, to make their task of reading easier and more pleasant, as well as a way of attracting and holding their attention and making a good impression. Messy or poorly laid-out writing can be more difficult to read, and can interfere with the transmission of our message. In extreme cases of poor presentation, we may not attempt to read the writing at all.

Attractive presentation is not usually intended for the writer; it is for the reader. This makes the audience its primary motivation. The intended purpose and audience will also dictate the kind of presentation the writing needs. For example, a poster makes certain demands regarding size of print, colour, white space, illustration, and so on; a business letter requires a different focus.

Teaching the purpose of a final draft

✔ Doing a final draft of writing simply for it to sit in a school notebook, to get a better mark, because it was assigned for homework, or because this is what happens to every piece of writing, are not valid reasons. They are likely to teach children that "final draft" is a school subject, rather than part of the real world of writing. Teach children how to judge for themselves just how much drafting, editing, correctness and neatness are needed for each individual piece of writing that they do. This is part of teaching them to think and act as writers. A draft report on the nesting habits of birds, for example, may never reach "publication" stage. It could, however, if stored, serve as the model for a report on animal habitats for later publication. Reviewing earlier work in this way also shows children how much progress they have made.

✔ A final draft is usually for the reader rather than the writer. It is the public face of our writing, the one that will make an impression and communicate our message. Make sure that before asking children to work on a final draft they know where their writing will be seen, and by whom. For example, is it a letter to the newspaper, a sign to be displayed, a story to be published? Will it be read by a classmate, a parent, the rest of the school, someone they do not know? What will that audience expect to see?

✔ Children can also learn the purpose of a final draft from what they do not do. There is little point in making a final draft of a shopping list, a memo to oneself, research notes, or your own diary. We may make changes to these to keep them up to date and accurate, but recopying for no real purpose is a waste of time. By differentiating their writing according to purpose and audience, children will learn how much redrafting they need to do. We can then expect them to make every effort to do a good, final draft when necessary.

✔ Do not be concerned that leaving much of their writing in early draft stage will teach children bad habits. As long as they know why some of their writing will stay messy and even incomplete, there should be no problem. Reassure parents that you are not neglecting the skills of presentation. You are teaching children when and where they are appropriate, and ensuring they learn and practice these skills in real situations.

✔ Give children honest feedback when they do a final draft. If a letter is not neat enough to post to a stranger, or a poem is too illegible to be displayed on the wall, tell the writer so. If there are still spelling mistakes, suggest someone to help with proofreading and editing. If the handwriting is not the best the child can do, say, "This is not up to your usual standard. Do you really want other people to see this?" You can do this in a constructive way by offering help to upgrade the draft.

✔ Children need to know what standard is expected for different kinds of writing. This standard may not be the same for all the children. Form your expectations according to the best each child is able to do; this will give each child a reasonable chance for success.

✔ Set up a kit for final draft writing. The kit could contain such items as different colours and sizes of pens and markers, good-quality paper, erasers, and book covers. Using these will emphasize the fact that final-draft writing is different, and is worth an extra effort.

Printing and handwriting

Every official form we fill in asks the writer to print in block capitals. It would seem that adult handwriting cannot be relied upon to be legible. This is because most adults have only one handwriting mode that they use in every situation. In fact, we need two different handwriting skills: speed and style. These are usually mutually exclusive; the faster we write, the more our style suffers, in some cases resulting in handwriting that is barely legible even to the writer.

As in all other aspects of writing, children need to learn what to focus on in different writing situations. Style and speed are both important, neither being the more desirable. What the writer must decide is which is appropriate in different situations.

Strategies for teaching printing and handwriting

✔ Some letters are made up of straight lines, some are curved lines, and some have a combination of straight lines and curves. Beginning writers can learn and practice letter shapes in these groups.

✔ When they are first learning letters, the children can use different media to create the shapes: they can draw them in sand or finger paint, form them with plasticine, clay, pipe-cleaners, and so on.

✔ You can draw children's attention to the features of letters by providing materials with which to make straight lines, circles and curves – for example, toothpicks, popsicle sticks, washers, coins, bingo chips, pipe-cleaners, string and so on. Challenge the children to make as many letters as they can using only straight lines, or only circles, or any combinations of the three shapes.

✔ As soon as possible, let children practice printing and writing whole words, phrases and sentences, rather than just individual letters. If they copy a poem, a joke, or an address, and do not have to compose sentences at the same time, or worry about how to spell the words, then they will be able to focus totally on their pencraft.

✔ When children are trying to develop language to express thoughts and ideas, it is too much to ask them to concentrate on handwriting at the same time. Take short periods of time outside the composing process for children to practice handwriting. Sometimes this could be practicing specific skills, such as individual letters or strings of letters. Sometimes it might be copying a piece of writing for display. At this time, the child will be able to focus totally on the handwriting.

✔ When you examine the children's handwriting, note which features they do well, and which they do not; for example, individual letter shapes, joining letters, size, regularity, and slope. Praise what they do well, and direct their practice to those aspects they need to improve.

✔ The children can create collages for each letter by cutting out examples from newspapers and magazines. Posters and advertisements are particularly good for this, as they use many different shapes, styles, sizes and colours. This will draw children's attention to the many ways that letters can be used to create different results and effects.

✔ The best handwriting may be thought of as an art form with more to offer than just neatness. Show children examples of writing as art. Use an Art lesson for children to try different media for making letters. They could use a variety of paint, pastels, crayon and markers, and form letters in different sizes and orientations. They could try some illuminated capitals to start their own stories.

✔ The children could work in small groups to create alphabet books, each one using a different style to print the letters. Challenge them to come up with innovative ways to make letters. Once the children have enjoyed the books in their own classroom, they could present the books to a class of younger children, or place them in the school library.

✔ For those children who have good motor control, and who are interested, show them examples of italic script, and show them how to do it for themselves. They will find it easier to start with felt-tip markers with italic points, and with practice can perhaps move on to fountain pens. The slowness and care this kind of writing needs will stress the value of pencraft.

✔ Provide opportunities for the children to experiment with the fonts and sizes offered by a computer. This will show them how printing style can enhance their writing.

✔ Provide many opportunities for purposeful pencraft in the classroom. For example, the children can take turns to maintain a Current Events board, using school, local and national news.

✔ Let the children put up any signs, labels and notices that the classroom needs. Teach them to do a first draft on scrap paper, revise and edit, then plan their final draft.

✔ Set up a display board where the children can put up poems, sayings and jokes for others to read. Accept for display only final-draft pieces with a child's best effort at printing or handwriting.

✔ When the children keep their own records, such as books they have read or topics they have written about, make this a place for their best handwriting.

✔ Set up a Greetings Committee to monitor children's birthdays, and write a special greeting on the board or noticeboard on the right day. This committee can also send Get Well messages when a child or teacher is away for a length of time.

✔ Ask the children to bring in samples of handwriting from home. Rather than ask people to write a sample, they can bring in envelopes, letters, telephone messages, and so on. They can then display, discuss and analyze the handwriting skills. This can help to raise the children's awareness of what features make for good pencraft, and also show that many different styles can be legible and attractive. Most of the children will probably be able to produce better quality writing than the adults in their lives. Talk with the children about privacy issues before doing this exercise. They should always ask the author's permission before sharing writing that is not their own.

Choosing a format

Beginning writers are likely to make all their writing look the same. They are learning in reading that writing goes from left to right along the lines and from the top to the bottom of the page, and their writing will be doing the same.

As they become more sophisticated in their reading and writing, they will learn that different kinds of writing demand different formats. For example, a paragraph about what you were going to buy at the supermarket would be very difficult to follow; a vertical list is better.

Raising the children's awareness of different formats for writing

✔ Demonstrate the use of different formats. For example, make a list of jobs to be done today, a chart showing the week's timetable, all capital letters on a poster, a flow chart as an outline.

✔ Look at different formats in reading and discuss them with the children. Advertisements are excellent for this. For example, newspaper advertisements are written with incomplete sentences and as many abbreviations as possible. Look at magazine advertisements, and note how they use size and style of print, colour and pictures.

✔ Set writing tasks that will require different formats, and discuss the possibilities with the children. For example, in Science would a chart be a good way to record how beans are growing?

✔ Research reports provide good opportunities for learning about formats. The children can make decisions about titles, side headings, underlining, indented paragraphs, and so on.

The computer in the drafting process

No matter how poor our handwriting, a computer printout looks the same for everyone; it is the great leveller. With a keyboard, even beginning writers can make their writing look perfect. Children who are reluctant to write because their writing is slow or always looks messy may be encouraged to write more with a keyboard. The greatest feature of writing with a computer is that the writing is not printed for public viewing until the author says it is ready. It is also a perfect model of the drafting process, because it makes changing the text so easy. As computers become more accessible in classrooms, children can learn to store draft material on disk on a personal electronic workpad or laptop. Recent "voice-type" programs can also be helpful for children whose keyboard skills are limited, but you need to review these carefully since price often reflects quality.

The computer becomes less useful when children can compose faster than they can type, and when they want to write lengthy pieces. Then the keyboard can inhibit the flow of ideas and language. If computers are available for children to use frequently for writing, then it is worth taking the time to teach correct keyboarding skills. Consider making typing lessons an after-school option for children (and adults) who are interested, and particularly those who have access to a computer at home. You may find a parent or a student who will volunteer to do this training.

Classroom assistants and volunteers can often help by acting as secretary to type in children's ideas. This is best done while the child is present so that the decisions on editing, cutting and pasting are made by the author.

Chapter

6

Different kinds of writing

When young children first start writing, they often express themselves just as they would when speaking. As they mature as readers and writers, the children will discover that there are many different kinds of writing, and a writer needs to adapt the writing genre to suit the purpose and audience.

As we have already seen, the three main categories of writing are:

✔ Expressive or personal writing
✔ Transactional or information-bearing writing
✔ Poetic or literary writing.

Expressive writing

Expressive language is a resource the children bring with them to school, and their first writing is much like talk written down. Young writers write about themselves, what they like, what they do, what is important to them. They write for themselves, their families, their friends. They use their own vocabulary, their own speech patterns, their own style.

Children often use expressive writing for the same purposes as talk: to relate personal anecdotes, to give opinions, to record their feelings, to explain their actions. Expressive writing is not necessarily all about personal experiences, but it does reflect experience from the writer's point of view. As we grow older, we still keep this kind of writing for such things as personal letters, diaries, messages and notes to ourselves. It is not intended for an audience, at least not one that is critical of our style. It tends to be first-draft writing, having little purpose for revision and editing.

Since expressive writing is closest to our own thoughts and language, it is the mode we use to frame new thoughts, to solve problems, to explore new learning, to think through our ideas. The most important aspect of expressive writing is the writer's own thoughts and ideas. Explaining something in our own words is often a good test of whether or not we really understand it. "In your own words" is a good summary of expressive writing. This makes expressive writing important in content-area subjects, where children are dealing with new facts and information.

Expressive writing is the starting point for children's later writing development. It is important that, as they continue through school, they still have many opportunities for expressive writing in all subject areas.

Examples of expressive writing

✔ Personal letter   ✔ Journal   ✔ E-mail   ✔ Memo
✔ Diary   ✔ Memoir   ✔ Joke

Opportunities for expressive writing

✔ Provide each child with a notebook to use as a response journal. Writing reflections down in a journal is one way of clarifying thoughts, setting goals and expectations, and working out what you have learned. At first, you can prompt journal entries with specific questions; as they gain experience, the children will no longer need the prompts. They can use the journal at any time of the day and in any subject.

✔ Writing in role as a character in history is a good way for children to personalize factual information.

✔ Writing in role as a character in literature will help children to put themselves inside a story, and better understand feelings and emotions. It will also help them to read for detail and subtext.

Monday 19 October
Today I planted a bean. I put wet paper towel around the inside of a jar, and slipped the bean down the side. The bean is dark reddish brown with light spots on it.

Tuesday 20 October
I checked the bean, but nothing had changed. I'd better make sure the paper towel doesn't dry out.

Thursday 22 October
The shell of the bean is starting to split open. This could be the roots on their way.

✔ The children can keep a journal to record a science experiment. They can record not only their observations, but their questions and predictions.

✔ Some children may like to keep a diary. Be wary of making this a daily requirement. Children's lives are not filled with constant excitement and interest, so a diary can become a chore and the writing dull and repetitive. If children have a response journal, they can use this to write an account or a reaction when something interesting occurs.

✔ Before a group or class discussion, ask the children to jot down their ideas and opinions in preparation. They can refer to these as the discussion progresses. Afterwards, the children can throw their papers away. Once they know this kind of writing will not be read, corrected, evaluated or marked, the children will feel free to use this risk-free opportunity for exploratory writing.

✔ Set up an informal book-review binder. After reading a book, the children can write their opinions and file them for future readers. For this kind of writing, they should not be restricted to any set format or length, but just write what they feel.

✔ Set aside an area of the noticeboard for editorials. Children can write what they think about any issue they choose, and post their writing on the board. Other children can then respond, and add their writing to the display. Do not interfere with this writing, except to keep within the bounds of kindness and propriety; it must be risk-free to be effective.

Transactional writing

Transactional writing deals with facts and information. It is used to record information, to report on events, to give instructions and directions, to make comparisons, to explain, to persuade.

In transactional writing, it is very important that all the facts are included and correct. It is also important that the information is organized well, so that it is accessible to a reader.

Different kinds of transactional writing require different formats and styles; sometimes a list or chart is more appropriate than a paragraph. Certain subjects have their own conventions for recording information; a science experiment is not recorded in the same way as a weather forecast, for example.

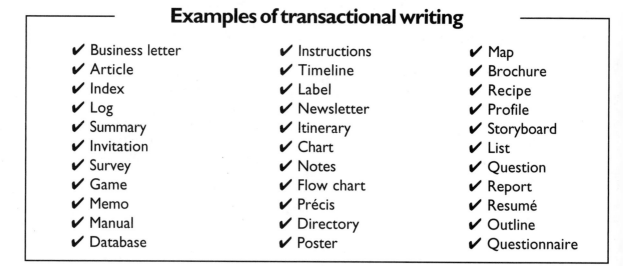

Examples of transactional writing

✔ Business letter	✔ Instructions	✔ Map
✔ Article	✔ Timeline	✔ Brochure
✔ Index	✔ Label	✔ Recipe
✔ Log	✔ Newsletter	✔ Profile
✔ Summary	✔ Itinerary	✔ Storyboard
✔ Invitation	✔ Chart	✔ List
✔ Survey	✔ Notes	✔ Question
✔ Game	✔ Flow chart	✔ Report
✔ Memo	✔ Précis	✔ Resumé
✔ Manual	✔ Directory	✔ Outline
✔ Database	✔ Poster	✔ Questionnaire

Poetic writing

Poetic writing is language in its most polished form, language which is intended for an audience, often one that is unknown. Poetic language is designed to have an impact on the reader, to stir emotions, thoughts and opinions as well as to convey information; to make us laugh, cry or tremble on cue. Propaganda is an example of poetic writing, concerned more with influencing and persuading than with facts and truth. For this reason, the poetic writer needs to have control and power over language, and know how to use it to manipulate the reader. Poetic writing often goes through extensive revision, as the writer searches for the exact word or phrase. The most important aspect of poetic writing is its impact on the reader.

Types of poetic writing

✔ Story	✔ Argument	✔ Comic strip	✔ Song
✔ Description	✔ Poem	✔ Script	✔ Dialogue
✔ Title	✔ Biography	✔ Caption	✔ Obituary
✔ Jingle	✔ Autobiography	✔ Riddle	✔ Parody

Teaching poetic writing through patterning from literature

Literature provides children with some of the best examples of poetic language. Children can often use this language as a model for writing of their own. As they use the vocabulary and sentence structure they meet in their reading, they can gain a better understanding and appreciation of the special conventions of written language.

Patterning from literature will not only help the children in their own writing, but will make reading literature more predictable, and therefore more fluent. Using literary devices, such as alliteration or metaphor, in their own writing can give children a better appreciation of the literature they read.

You can help the children to learn to pay attention to particular aspects of writing, such as choice of words and sentence structure, by your choice of subjects for patterning, as the following examples will illustrate. As the children work in small groups or as a whole class to collect words and formulate language, they will hear and write the patterns many times, thus becoming more familiar with poetic language. This will give them many more resources to use in their own writing.

To follow a pattern, first read the selection with the children, and help them to note the patterns. Demonstrate the patterning by writing one or two examples yourself, then ask children to contribute ideas. Children who quickly grasp the pattern will provide more examples, and hearing these will help the other children to internalize the pattern and understand what they are to do. Children can then build their own patterned writing. Their products will often be suitable for publishing in an anthology, combining to make a larger product, or illustrating for a display.

Literary patterning techniques

Repetitive sentence pattern

Who Has Seen the Wind? By Christina Rossetti

Who has seen the wind?
Neither I nor you;
But when the leaves hang trembling
The wind is passing through.

Who has seen the wind?
Neither you nor I;
But when the leaves bow down their heads,
The wind is passing by.

A patterning model

✔ Use the phrase "when the leaves hang trembling" as a model.

✔ Ask the children to suggest other objects that might move in the wind. List the words on the board.

✔ Ask the children each to choose a word from the list, and substitute it for "leaves" in the original sentence; then they can add a suitable ending.

When hats blow along the gutter
When the trees bend low
When the clouds scud across the sky
I can see the wind.

✔ Combine the sentences in groups of three, and add the sentence "I can see the wind" to form the final line. You will now have a number of four-line poems which you can combine to form a longer poem.

Selecting one line or sentence for patterning will remove the necessity of rhyming, which is very difficult, and tends to restrict the vocabulary and language children can use.

You can add a new dimension to this pattern by changing the final line. Try, for example, "I can hear the wind." By changing the final line, you can use this same pattern for many other topics.

When the children go back to school
When the swimming pool closes
When warm sweaters come out of the cupboard
I know summer is over.

A predictable sequence

Traditional rhyme		Rhyme by class age 6	
A was an Apple Pie		*A is an Airplane*	
B bit it		*B built it*	
C cut it		*C cleaned it*	
D dealt it		*D dusted it*	
E eats it		*E exited it*	
F fought for it		*F flew it*	
G got it		*G grabbed it*	
H had it		*H helped it*	
I inspected it		*I de-iced it*	
J joined for it		*J jinxed it*	
K kept it		*K kicked it*	
L longed for it		*L lived in it*	
M mourned for it		*M moved it*	
N nodded at it		*N nudged it*	
O opened it		*O organized it*	
P peeped in it		*P papered it*	
Q quartered it		*Q questioned it*	
R ran for it		*R radioed it*	
S stole it		*S sang to it*	
T took it		*T travelled in it*	
U upset it		*V videoed it*	
V viewed it		*W waved to it*	
W wanted it		*X X-rayed it*	
X Y Z and ampersand		*Y yelled at it*	
All wished for a piece in hand.		*Z zoomed into the sky.*	

A patterning model

✔ First, ask the children to suggest other words for A. They can complete the sentence, "A is an _____" in different ways. List their suggestions on the board.

✔ Discuss which ones the children could use to build an alphabet, and which do not provide enough scope for ideas. For example, you can do many things with an airplane, but not so many with an aardvark.

✔ Ask the children to work in groups, each group choosing a different subject.

✔ Each group can produce a new alphabet, with an illustration for each letter. They can compile these into a book, with title page and authors' names.

✔ After enjoying their books in the classroom for a while, each group could take its book to another class to read aloud, then leave it for the classroom library.

Cumulative story

This is the house that Jack built

This is the malt
That lay in the house that Jack built

This is the rat
That ate the malt
That lay in the house that Jack built ...

It continues in this way until the climax:

This is the farmer sowing his corn
That fed the cock that crowed in the morn
That waked the priest all shaven and shorn
That married the man all tattered and torn,
That kissed the maiden all forlorn
That milked the cow with the crumpled horn
That tossed the dog
That worried the cat
That killed the rat
That ate the malt
That lay in the house that Jack built.

A patterning model

✔ It is not necessary to pattern a complete poem, especially one this long. You may choose to select certain recognizable and manageable portions. This model uses the rhyming couplet model, and ends with a model of the initial pattern. The children will necessarily make many false starts with ideas that they cannot sustain, and have to abandon them. This is an important piece of learning about the writing process, particularly as it relates to poetic writing; poetic writing demands careful consideration of words and language to make sure they are the best ones you can use.

✔ Draw the children's attention to the rhyming couplets in the poem. You can do this through choral reading, assigning couplets to different groups or individuals. The rhyme remains the same throughout the original, but this is difficult and it is not necessary to maintain this.

✔ Help the children to note how each new idea builds on the former to create a continuous story.

✔ Choose a new topic, one that will allow for many different "ingredients": This is the cake that Jason made; This is the bus we ride on; This is the tree we climb up; This is the ship that Drake sailed.

✔ Start by patterning the first few verses until you have about five lines.

✔ Next work on several rhyming couplets, and add them at the beginning of the poem.

The Library in Our School

These are the children, a special breed,
Who come to the library eager to read.

This is the librarian helping them choose
Poems and legends, fables and news.

These are the heroes brave and bold,
That belong in the stories new and old,

That inhabit the chapters
That make up the books
That sit on the shelves
That line the walls
That surround the library in our school.

More patterning techniques

Idea patterning

You can use an idea from a selection or from a theme, and give children a framework to write from. This may help them to identify with and respond personally to characters and situations.

--- **Examples** ---

Now and Then

When I was little I _____
But now _____

When I was little, I was pushed in a baby carriage.
But now I push the pedals of my own bike.

(Age 6)

Good News – Bad News

I like _____

I don't like _____

I like winter

when I am careering downhill on my toboggan.

I don't like winter

when I am shovelling snow from the path.

(Age 10)

Comparatives

A _____ is funny
A _____ is funnier
A _____ is the funniest thing I know

A clown is funny.
A Road Runner cartoon is funnier.
Dad falling into the river is the funniest
thing I've seen.

(Age 8)

Consequences

Hello _____
Goodbye _____

Hello skateboard.
Goodbye knees!

(Age 10)

Form poetry	A form poem is a frame or model for writing poetry. A limerick is a classic example of a form poem; all limericks start in a similar way, and follow the same pattern of syllables, stress, rhyme, number of lines, and so on. Because the word and sentence patterns are preset, children can focus on choosing just the right words to express thoughts and images.
Cinquain	Cinquain gets its name from its five lines. Each line has a specific shape and function:

Line 1	one word	title	*snowflake*
Line 2	two words	adjectives	*cold, white*
Line 3	three words	'ing' verbs	*drifting, swirling, tumbling*
Line 4	four words	statement, opinion	*makes my spirits rise*
Line 5	one word	first, or synonym	*crystal*

Diamante

This is much like a cinquain poem, but is more complex. Its name comes from the diamond shape it creates. A diamante moves from a word to its antonym or other extreme. The real skill is to make the transition in the centre line as seamless as possible, so one opposite glides into the other.

Line 1 one word title	*Summer*
Line 2 two adjectives	*languid, lethargic*
Line 3 three verbs	*golfing, swimming, gardening*
Line 4 four adjectives	*welcome, fleeting, ominous, frustrating,*
Line 5 three verbs	*slipping, sliding, shovelling*
Line 6 two adjectives	*biting, numbing*
Line 7 antonym of title	*winter*

Haiku and tanka

These are classical Japanese forms that are quite difficult to write. Make sure children hear and read many examples before trying to write their own.

A haiku is written in 17 syllables and three lines, and makes one statement, usually about nature.

Line 1 five syllables	*I trudge through the storm,*
Line 2 seven syllables	*my senses reeling wildly,*
Line 3 five syllables	*fighting for my breath.*

If you add to this two lines of seven syllables each, then you have a tanka poem:

Line 4 seven syllables	*Safety is attainable;*
Line 5 seven syllables	*home looms comfortably close.*

Free-form model

To help children to write a free-form poem, establish a pattern and purpose for each line:

Title	*A Day at the Beach*
Subject	*Carefree children*
Action	*Swim, surf and shout*
Where	*Along the water's edge*
Why	*Holidays have begun*

The children can follow this structure and use ideas and information from their reading.

Title	Relief in munchkinland
Subject	Dorothy and the Munchkins
Action	Dance, Sing, cheer
Where	Along the Yellow Brick Road.
Why	The wicked witch is dead!

Starter words

To generate and explore ideas about a topic, children can write a series of sentences starting with the subject word. It can be an object, a feeling or any kind of word you choose. This can be a way for children to express their feelings about characters or ideas in their reading. You may wish to suggest a minimum and maximum number of lines that the children write, perhaps four to eight. After sharing their ideas, each child could then contribute one line to a group poem. This will reinforce the concept of selecting your very best from a number of attempts.

Ideas for starter words

Start with a noun

Cyclones come from nowhere.
Cyclones reduce houses to nothing.   (Age 9)

Start with an abstract noun

Happiness is the open road.
Happiness is having friends like Ratty and Mole.   (Age 8)

Start with an adverb

Suddenly, Lucy spotted the wardrobe.
Cautiously, she stepped inside.
Boldly, she decided to explore.   (Age 10)

Sensory poems

To write a sensory poem, the children choose an object, a place, season, and so on, and describe it using each of their senses. If they choose an idea from their reading, they will need to reread to select specific information. Looking at a scene or handling an object can help children to generate words and ideas; they can look out of the window at a snowstorm, stand out in the wind, study a photograph or hold a kitten.

To help them to organize their words and ideas into a poem, you can give them a frame such as the one below. Write the final line first, to set the topic. Once the children are used to using this frame, you can give them a blank to use to guide their ideas and language.

Frame for sensory poem

1 (sense)	2 (starter)	3 (objects)	4 (what are they doing?)
Sight	I can see		
Hearing	I can hear		
Touch	I can feel		
Smell	I can smell		
Taste	I can taste		
Reason			

1 (sense)	2 (starter)	3 (objects)	4 (what are they doing?)
Sight	I can see	*leaves*	*falling from the trees*
Hearing	I can hear	*birds*	*planning their journey south*
Touch	I can feel	*wind*	*brushing my cheeks*
Smell	I can smell	*smoke*	*curling from chimneys*
Taste	I can taste	*apples*	*melting on my tongue*
Reason		*Autumn is here*	

When you have used the frame to build the poem, use only columns 3 and 4 for the finished product. Sometimes not all the senses are appropriate to a chosen topic. In this case children can choose three of the five senses for a shorter poem.

	September
(I can see)	*Buses and cars arriving at the gate*
(I can hear)	*Children calling to one another across the playground*
(I can feel)	*Excitement building everywhere*
(Reason)	*We're back to school!*

Similes

This is a model for a descriptive poem. The children will readily learn the term "simile" if you link it with "similar" and use this kind of patterning to make comparisons.

First choose a noun, perhaps suggested by a story, and ask the children to write a list of adjectives to describe it. If they do this in small groups, they will have many more words from which to choose later.

Give the children a frame using the word "like":

_____ like a _____

The children can then try each of their adjectives in the first blank, and try to finish each sentence with a comparison.

The poems tend to sound better and have closure if you put the title at the end.

Noisy	*like*	*an express train*
Destructive	*like*	*an explosion*
Frightening	*like*	*an intruder*
Tornado.		

These can remain as individual four-line poems, or you can combine the similes to create a longer, group poem.

Comparisons

This is another model for descriptive writing. Choose a word, an image, a person from a story, and ask the children to write statements of comparison. You can start children off by collecting some of the well-known and over-used ones, and asking children to continue the pattern with ideas of their own.

as	*quiet*	*as*	*a mouse*
as	*cunning*	*as*	*a fox*
as	_____	*as*	_____

Chapter

7

Providing an audience

You will most likely be the main audience for the children's writing. As often as possible, you will give the children feedback while their writing is still in progress. At this time, you can help them to learn new skills and techniques. As editor-in-chief of the classroom publishing company, you will be the final arbiter of what is up to publishing standard and what is not. The writing you choose to publish or display will set the standard for excellence.

It is important also to provide other audiences, both inside and outside the classroom. The children need to feel that other people are interested in what they are writing about.

Writing partners

The most useful response to writing takes place while the writing is still in progress. Initial audience feedback can let the writer know how successful the writing is, and what changes might be made to make it better. A "fresh eye" can often help us to see where our writing is not clear, not complete or not interesting. A writing partner can help with writing-in-progress by becoming a partner in the writing process, reviewing the work with a sympathetic but objective eye.

Using writing partners

✔ Assign regular writing partners. This could be a pair or three children who work together on a regular basis. As the children work together, they will develop trust in one another, and this can help to establish a "writers' workshop" atmosphere.

✔ Mixed-ability groups are usually more productive, as there will be a wider range of skills. Even the children who are less fluent writers can often give valuable feedback as listeners, and learn about how to make their own writing better at the same time.

✔ You can provide a regular time for writing partners to work together. This could be at the end of the writing period, or at designated times during the week. Alternatively, groups can initiate their own meetings as the need arises.

✔ When the children first start working with partners, give them some guidelines about what to talk about. For example:

- Listen to, or read, the writing
- Say one thing you liked about it
- Ask the writer a question about the content
- Make a suggestion about what might make it better.

Once the children are used to talking to each other about their writing, they will not need these prompts.

✔ As writing partners talk to each other, you can circulate round the groups, listen in on discussions, model the kinds of questions and comments that are productive, give helpful suggestions and generally monitor how the groups are functioning.

✔ Children who are less than fluent readers often manage remarkably well when reading another child's writing. Children with specific learning disabilities are often able to give advice and support, even though they may be unable to put this advice into practice themselves. Being able to help can give these children confidence and self-esteem, and earn them the respect of their peers.

✔ Children can help one another with proofreading and editing even when their own knowledge is limited. Most children can be proficient at some aspect of editing, even if it is only to be a second pair of eyes.

The writers' circle

Provide a time, perhaps once a week, for the children to share a piece of writing with the whole class.

One teacher who initiated a writers' circle was surprised how gentle and supportive the children were with less than accomplished first attempts. On one occasion a child was so carried away by the excitement of his own story that his fingers fumbled as he turned the page. The bated breath with which the children waited for him to proceed was an immediate lesson in the power of suspense. Other children learned to enjoy adding elements to their story to make their audience laugh.

✔ Ask the children to sign up ahead of time if they would like to participate in the writers' circle. This will let you know how much time it will take.

✔ You may need to limit the time each child reads, perhaps to five minutes. This will allow more children to participate, and also avoid the boredom of run-on stories. The children will have to select their very best, and this can focus their attention on what kind of audience response they are likely to get.

✔ Only volunteers should participate. Oral reading can be highly stressful for some children, and is not then a learning experience. You can keep a record of those who do not take part, and provide other opportunities for them to share their writing.

✔ You could also ask the children to work in two or three groups to give more of them a chance to share.

Parents as audience

To be a helpful and supportive audience, parents need to understand the writing process, and the kinds of priorities each stage has. If they do not understand, their response can often focus on secretarial kinds of skills, rather than authorship issues. Spelling and neatness are the most visible aspects of writing, but an undue emphasis on these at the wrong time can discourage the child and make risk-taking unlikely.

One effective idea tried by a teacher was periodically to send home children's writing folders to be "sorted and tidied". The children could store pieces for future reference, discard work they felt was not up to standard or no longer needed, and order their work to show how they had progressed. All the work in the folder was unmarked. The children were encouraged to discuss this sorting with their parents. Parents could see what work had been undertaken, and select gems they felt were worthy of displaying or sharing at home. Parents also became partners in their children's writing, helping them to find more information. The children's retained work was much tidier when stored in the classroom, and less of it was discarded on the sidewalk on the way home.

✔ Bring parents into the classroom as helpers whenever possible, even if only for one writing period. In this way they can learn how you work with the children, and what kinds of responses are productive.

✔ Encourage the children to write "First Draft" on their early writing. Make sure the children understand what is involved in a first draft, and what is not a focus at this time. They can then explain this to their parents when they are sharing their writing at home. You can model this by writing "first draft" on the board when you are writing for the children, or during a guided writing session. This gives you the freedom to cross out and change, and use less than your neatest handwriting.

✔ From time to time, send home first, intermediate and final drafts together. Ask the children to explain to their parents how they progressed from start to finish.

✔ Send home some guidelines for parents, suggesting how they might respond to first and final draft writing. For example:

Guidelines for parents

A first draft is a collection of your child's initial ideas for a piece of writing. It is work in progress. The ideas have not yet been organized or proofread. When you read your child's first-draft writing:

✔ Show an interest in the content

✔ Ask questions about anything you didn't understand

✔ Be supportive, and encourage your child to continue

✔ Give any help your child asks for

✔ Ignore spelling and neatness; they are not a focus at this time.

A final draft is a finished piece of writing, ready for an audience. It represents the best your child can do at this stage. When you read your child's final-draft writing:

✔ Show an interest in the content

✔ Praise the child's achievements

✔ Note how the writing is presented: handwriting and neatness

✔ Make judgments about the writing in terms of what your child is capable of doing

✔ Help your child to feel encouraged to write again.

An outside audience

✔ Extend the writers' circle idea by enabling the children to share their writing with a larger audience at an assembly. Make sure the children are well-rehearsed and that their time is strictly controlled.

✔ Encourage the children to write voluntary book reviews to be displayed in the school or classroom library. You can provide a blank form to use as a structure for this.

✔ The children can write stories for younger children. They can visit another class and read their stories aloud, or publish books to be given to the other class.

✔ Your day-to-day activities will provide many opportunities for letter writing. Children can write to companies or agencies asking for information for projects; to a local councillor or politician; to a local newspaper; to pen pals in another school. Children can also take over the writing of letters and memos to be sent home. You can usually find company mailing addresses on websites.

✔ Publish a class or school newspaper. In preparation, the children can read national and local newspapers, plan sections and divide up the writing task. Through your local newspaper, you can obtain supplements, competitions, and fact sheets aimed specifically at schools. Producing a newspaper is a major undertaking, and might be assigned to one year in the school, with several classes working together. This will increase the amount of collaboration and feedback the children will be involved in.

✔ The children can make signs, labels and captions for the classroom. One child in kindergarten was fascinated by the "Now wash your hands" sign she had seen in public toilets, so she made her own version for the school washroom. A sign, however abbreviated, has to go through the stages of the writing process: establish purpose and audience, decide on content and wording, plan layout and effective size and lettering, and make an attractive final draft. Here are some ideas:

  – Rules for using centres
  – How many people can work here
  – Lists of names
  – Editor-of-the-day
  – Daily timetable
  – Daily date
  – Today's weather
  – Instructions
  – Labels for cupboard doors showing what is stored there
  – Names on coat hooks.

Chapter 8

Assessment and record-keeping

Do not think you have to evaluate and respond to all the writing that children do. If you can read and respond to all the writing done in your classroom, the children are probably not writing enough. The learning is primarily in doing the writing, with a little help along the way, rather than in receiving a score at the end of it. Regard much of the children's writing as "practice". Then plan a manageable scheme for detailed assessment.

The approach to assessment

You can develop a two-stage assessment scheme:

✔ Each time you read the children's writing, decide on one aspect you will assess and respond to. You might look only at completeness of content, complexity of sentences, paragraphing, or neatness. The aspect you focus on might reflect specific skills you have been teaching. This will indicate how each child performs on specific skills.

✔ From time to time, take one piece of writing, and evaluate the children's level of ability in all aspects of the writing process: content, organization, spelling, punctuation, presentation. You could use perhaps one narrative and one transactional piece per month. This will indicate how the children integrate all the skills of writing, and use the writing process to bring a piece to completion.

Each time you make an assessment, you can add information to your records.

To make sure there is consistency throughout the school, you could work together to develop some guidelines for assessing writing in all classes and in all subject areas. For example:

✔ Assess the writing according to the stages of the writing process
✔ Relate your assessment and comments to the purpose of the writing
✔ Evaluate only what was the focus of the task
✔ Keep checklists of specific skills.

Responding to writing

A response to writing can be positive or negative. It can also be constructive or non-constructive.

Writing "Good work" on a child's writing is a positive comment, and will make the child feel good. However, it is non-constructive. It does not say in what respect the work was good, so does not help the child to repeat the experience.

Writing "This is not up to your usual standard" is a negative comment. It also is non-constructive, as it does not specify what is lacking.

Marks and grades alone are likely to be non-constructive. Unless we get 100%, we need to know where we went wrong. Without this knowledge, the writer will not know how to improve next time. Without this knowledge, the teacher will not know what kinds of help and instruction the child needs.

Comments do not have to be positive all the time. There is nothing wrong with telling a child that a piece of writing is not good; the child has a right to know. But to be really helpful, comments must be specific and tell the child what was good and what was not. We must then follow this up with appropriate help and instruction.

Negative responses can be very helpful, as long as they are offered in a spirit of partnership, and do not discourage the writer or reduce self-esteem. "Teacher as partner in dialogue" is one of the more productive relationships for teaching writing. "I don't understand that part" could be the most helpful thing you can say to a writer.

However, a comment is most constructive if it comes while the writing is in progress; then the writer has a chance to rectify the situation before final-draft stage. Responding to audience feedback is one of the best ways to improve writing.

When you read a piece of writing, have in mind two lists:

✔ What you expect the writing to be like.
✔ What the individual child is capable of producing.

Assess the writing according to these two criteria. You can then respond in a way that is both honest and helpful.

You can also respond according to the skills of the drafting process:

Text level	meaning and content
	organizing information, sequencing, paragraphing
Sentence level	sentence structure and grammar
	style, effective use of language
Word level	vocabulary
	spelling
Presentation	punctuation, neatness, handwriting

Try to comment specifically on the writer's achievement or lack of success in each of these four areas.

Record-keeping

You can also use this framework for your own record-keeping of each child's level of achievement.

Name	David Watson				
Date	**Assignment**	**Text Level**	**Sentence Level**	**Word Level**	**Presentation**
9 Oct	Personal anecdote	Detailed Sequenced No paragraphs	Short, simple, repetitive patterns	Errors in high-frequency words	Neat Upper and lower case not consistent periods No commas No speech marks

This may seem time-consuming, but it does not have to be this thorough for every piece of writing. You could use the two-stage assessment scheme referred to on p. 66.

✔ With most pieces of writing, choose only one of these columns for focus. Read the writing for that aspect primarily, and make comments on that focus only. This will enable you to build up over time a picture of each child's strengths and weaknesses. You can use this information to plan instruction, and perhaps to form special instructional groups.

✔ A few times a year, perhaps before the end of each term, take one piece of writing and assess the child's proficiency at all four levels. You can use this information to assess a child's level of achievement in each area.

Writing assessment portfolios

A portfolio is a record of the child's best work. It will enable you to keep track of growth and change, and also look back over a child's work over a long period of time. At any time, you can use the portfolio to assess knowledge and growth, update your records, and report to parents and administrators.

We want the children to experiment, to try new techniques, to practice new skills. This will result in many failed pieces of writing, many false starts, many dummy runs, as well as many successes. We cannot fairly assess a child's competence in writing by looking at an average of all the work. Skill level may more accurately be judged by looking at the best a child can do.

About once a month, sort through the folders with the children, and clear them out. Decide what the child will take home, and what will be discarded. At this time, choose a piece that is representative of the best work the child can do. Keep this yourself in a separate file to build the portfolio. Whenever possible, keep all drafts of a piece of writing. Share this writing with parents at a Parents' Evening, and refer to them when you write your reports.

At the end of the year, choose three pieces from each portfolio to keep as a permanent record; one from early in the year, one from midway and one from the end. Make a photocopy if necessary, so that the child can keep the originals. You can pass these on to the child's next teacher to help in reporting the child's level of achievement. In your school, you can thus keep a portfolio for each child from kindergarten to leaving. No test, anecdotal record or checklist will give you as much accurate information about a child's growth in all the skills of writing as actual samples of the child's work over a number of years.

Chapter

9

Classroom publishing

A broad definition of "publishing" is putting writing on display for others to read. This will provide the range of audiences that gives children the motivation they need for writing, revision, editing, and presentation. The ultimate product is a bound book. It is ideal if the children can each have several books published during the year, but because making books is time-consuming, it is good to have many other ways to display the children's writing.

Information about making different books, including pop-up books, is contained in *Making Books* by Paul Johnson (Pembroke, 2000).

Ways to display children's writing

Picture frames

Picture frames come in many sizes and shapes. You can choose some to hang on the wall, and some with stands to display on a table or shelf. Ask the children to bring in any old frames they have at home. Many picture frames have an easy-to-remove backing, so the display can be changed regularly.

You can make your own frames by cutting stiff cardboard to shape, and covering it with fabric, perhaps with a layer of padding underneath. Attach the writing behind the frame with pins, add a card to hold it stiff, and it is easily removed to change the display. Use a coloured or patterned mat to make a display look really special. The children may like to customise the frames with paint, or by pasting on seasonal or theme-related decorations.

Picture frames are ideal for writing that is no more than one page in length, such as short stories, poems, brief reports, handwriting samples. The frame helps to show writing as an art form, and may encourage children to develop their handwriting style. You can use large frames to build collages of writing, displaying many children's work together.

Concertina books

To make a concertina book, cut heavy paper or light card to shape, and join the required number of pages together with transparent tape. Attach two lengths of ribbon to the cover to tie the book together when it is not in use.

Use both sides for the writing, and arrange the leaves so that the story runs from left to right, with the title page on top and a blank page for the back cover.

You can display the concertina book standing open, then stack it on a book shelf with other books.

Photograph albums

Albums are designed to make adding and removing photographs quick and easy. The best kind to use have plastic covers for each page, so they will keep the writing neat and clean. Some albums are ring-binders, so you can add additional pages as you need them or take out extras.

Children can build their own individual albums in which to keep their final-draft writing. Work with them to choose their best pieces of writing, then help them to make a good, final draft. This will form their portfolio of best work, and is a good thing to take home from time to time, or to display at an Open Evening or Parents' Evening. They are also good for group projects, class anthologies, and other collections. The children can combine photographs and writing for a family history, autobiography, or holiday journal.

Plate stands

Commercial plate stands are usually made of wood or metal. You can make your own with heavy cardboard. Cut out several in different sizes, using coloured paper or cardboard. For a more decorative stand, cover a large sheet of cardboard on both sides with wallpaper or gift-wrapping paper, then cut out your forms. A simple fold down the centre is enough in light cardboard, but with heavy cardboard it works better if you cut down the fold and tape the join on both sides, leaving a small gap between the pieces.

To mount the writing, glue, staple or paper-clip it to stiff cardboard, then sit it on the stand. The stands fold flat for easy storage when not in use.

Cubes

A cube has six sides, so it can display six items. The cube can be any size you choose, although storage can be difficult with larger ones. Build the cube, then paste the items for display on the sides. If you cover the cube with plastic, you will be able to remove papers and reuse the cube. You can use wire coat-hangers and sewing thread and hang several cubes to make a mobile.

A cube can tell a story in six chapters, give a report on six aspects of a topic, display six poems on a similar theme, six pen portraits, six pictures and many other ideas. Paste a picture on one side, and add five pieces of descriptive writing. To guide a research project, the children can paste five questions on one side, and answer each question on one of the other sides.

Designing a piece of writing especially for a cube will involve children in pre-planning. It is a good opportunity to work on such skills as making outlines, choosing formats and prioritizing content to fit the space available. It is a good project for a group of five, each child being responsible for completing one side, with the remaining side left for the title and authors' names.

Clear plastic covers

These come in different sizes and are specifically designed to hold paper. The children will easily be able to slide their own pages in and out. They can then be filed upright in a box, pinned on the noticeboard, hung on a ring, punched for a ring-binder, or attached to the writing board with tape. They can also be placed on a table in the classroom library for other children to read.

Postcards

Postcards typically have a picture on one side and space to write a message on the reverse. You can purchase cards blank on both sides or use file cards, which come in many different sizes and colours. Completed cards file well, and are easy to store and retrieve in a shoebox. They also fit in some photograph albums with clear plastic inserts, so both sides can be read.

Postcards are an ideal format for short pieces of writing with an illustration. This could be a personal anecdote with a drawing, a cut-out picture with a piece of descriptive writing or a poem, instructions with a diagram, a photograph with a character profile or a local map with tourist information.

Greetings cards

Children can collect used cards and paste their own writing and illustration over the commercial message. Cards provide an opportunity for up to four pages of writing, and give children practice in planning and organizing space.

Large, stiff cards stand well on a shelf or mantelpiece, so are an ideal format for the children to use in order to display their writing at home. They can also send their writing to relatives by reusing greetings cards.

Ring-binders

Ring-binders make it easy to change, add, delete and reorganize writing. The children can make dividers, and sort and categorize the contents. They are ideal for group writing, enabling the children to compile anthologies, reports, word lists and many other kinds of information.

Building a ring-binder can be a model for the writing process, as items are first collected, then evaluated for relevance, categorized, sequenced and presented.

The children could keep personal ring-binders for their writing. In it, they could have sections for drafts in progress, finished writing, a "tomorrow file" (writing ideas), words (words to proofread for, theme words, interesting words to use), and any other notes relevant to their writing.

Display fold-out

You can create a cardboard fold-out display of any size, for a shelf, desk, table-top or to stand on the floor. The larger the display, the heavier the cardboard you will need. You can use any number of folding pieces, although three make a very stable, easy to read and easy to store model.

Ask a shop that sells large appliances or a supermarket to save some large boxes for you. Cut the cardboard to the size you want, and join the sides together with strong tape, front and back. For larger displays, book-binding tape is ideal; you will need to bind over all the corners to stop them fraying and bending. Leave enough space between the cardboard sheets so that the sides will fold flat; this makes storage and transportation easier. Your display board will last longer and stay cleaner if you cover it with plastic, and attach papers to it with two-sided or transparent tape.

When all the children have worked on a project and have reports, pictures and so on, they can assemble a large display, and put it outside the classroom for others to read. If you have enough room for children to walk all round it, you can use both sides of the board.

Dowel scroll

Use two lengths of dowelling or pieces of broom handle as the ends of a scroll. The dowel should be two or three inches longer than the paper at the top and bottom, so as to give the reader something to hold and turn. Either attach pages of the writing together side by side, or print the final draft in columns on paper that has been cut to the right length first. (This takes more planning, as the child will need to know exactly how much space will be needed.) Print the title and author's name along the outside edge. Roll the scroll from the end so that the beginning of the writing unrolls first. Add two ribbons at the opening edge to tie the scroll for storage.

Scrolls are particularly good for historical subjects, as they impart a sense of the past. For writing on ancient topics, the children can first stain the paper with cold tea, to achieve a parchment look.

Overhead transparencies

The children can paper-clip a transparency over a piece of lined paper with the lines as a guide, and write with a medium-point marker. Trial and error will show them what size is right for the intended audience, making this a good lesson in the value of a first draft.

This technique provides an interesting way for children to share factual information, such as the results of an interview or research project. They can show questions they asked, then read the answers; or summarize information, then orally add details. They can also show pictures with captions, comic strips, posters and advertisements.

The children can also illustrate a story on transparencies, and show them as they read the story aloud. This allows them to share their writing orally, and is a good opportunity for rehearsed oral reading.

If the children write and illustrate using non-permanent markers, the transparencies can easily be rinsed in warm water and reused.

Bound books

A bound book for the classroom or school library, or to present to a friend or family member, is the ultimate goal for classroom publishing. Parent volunteers can help with the construction aspects, and can also type the text for those children who cannot print their own.

Making books is time-consuming, but even if we had plenty of time, quantity is not the ultimate goal. One of the purposes of publishing is to demonstrate to children the value of revision, editing and presentation. You can best do this by choosing only the very best work for binding into real books. When a child has several suitable pieces, review them together and make a choice. At this time, the writing may go through some additional revision and editing. This selection process is an opportunity to talk with the children about their past writing, and what makes some writing better than others.

As a guideline, set a target of two or three books per year for each child, and supplement this with several other display methods. When you have trained some helpers, you may be able to increase this number, and the children can build up their own personal libraries of published books. As the children grow older, their books may change in character, and decrease in number. Rather than many small picture books, they may publish a year's collection of their best short stories, an anthology of poems, and a research report, for example.

How to bind books

Hard-cover books

To make the covers, you will need cardboard cut from supermarket boxes, wallpaper or fabric for a covering, and glue. Wallpaper sample books are often the right size for this and old ones are free.

1. Cut the cardboard a little larger than the intended page size – 16 x 23 cm (6½ × 9 in.) is a good size for folded paper.
2. Place two sheets side by side on the covering, leaving about a 1.5 cm (½ in.) gap between them. (This will allow the book to fold over and close. The more pages you plan to insert, the wider the gap must be.)
3. Cut the covering about 5 cm (2 in.) larger all round and cut across the corners.
4. Fold the covering over the cardboard and stick it down. If pre-pasted wallpaper is soaked first, it will not need extra glue.

To make the book pages, fold the required number of pages together and add one extra page on the outside. This will have nothing written on it and will eventually be stuck down to the front and back covers. Stitch through the centre with sewing thread. You will find stitching lasts longer than staples, as it does not tear the pages as easily. Leave the stitching and sticking until the child has completed the writing and illustrating; then mistakes can be more easily corrected.

Soft-cover books   Fold the required number of sheets of ordinary writing paper. You can vary the size and shape of books by the size of the original paper. Stitch through the centre with large loops of sewing thread, or staple top and bottom. You can add a coloured, thicker outside sheet for the cover.

Printing in this kind of book takes great care, as one mistake can spoil the whole effect. It is a good idea to leave the final stitching or stapling until the writing and illustrating are finished. This makes it easier to take out and replace a page that becomes spoiled.

This is a good way of teaching the importance of careful copying and neat, attractive printing. The children should only embark on this project when they have a fully edited and corrected piece of writing to copy, and when they have a reasonable chance of achieving a good result.

Larger-format books   Use one sheet of paper for each page. When the writing is complete, paste each page on construction paper or card, cutting a little larger all round to leave a border. Starting with the front cover, attach each page in turn by running transparent tape down the inside spine, finishing with the back cover. Bind the outside of the spine with book-binding tape.

If you laminate each page before sticking them together, you will produce a book that will stand up to many readings. The transparent tape will also become virtually invisible. Illustrations are best done with felt-tip markers, as crayon and coloured pencil marks often melt and smudge during the lamination process.

These books are time-consuming and more expensive to make, so this format is ideal for group writing, where a number of children collaborate on a story or report. As the pages can be very large, they are also good for picture books. Because each page is done separately, the children can complete the required pages, then put them in order, ready for assembly.

Whatever the means used to present their published work, the children themselves should take an active part in making at least some of the selection. Children might take turns to be part of a group responsible for presentation of written work in the classroom. This adds the extra element of *submitting* a piece for presentation to the publishing committee.

Appendix 1: Linking writing purposes to relevant forms

Purpose	Type of writing	Important features
To record feelings, observations, and so on	Personal letters; Reports; Poems; Notes and jottings; Diaries; Journals	Personal. Often need to be recorded as they occur. Abbreviated. May be revised or edited for an audience.
To describe	Character portraits Reports of sequences of events Labels and captions Advertisements	Often personal in first instance. Organization – may need cutting and pasting. May form part of a larger text for an audience.
To inform or advise	Posters; Scripts for news items; Minutes of meetings; Invitations; Programs; Information leaflets/flyers	Audience – immediate. Layout all-important. Need to be clear, neatly presented.
To persuade	Advertisements and commercials Letters to the Editor Notes for a debate Political cartoons	Audience – immediate. Layout all-important. Need to be clear, neatly presented.
To clarify thinking	Notes from research Charts, graphs, diagrams Jottings	Personal. Often need to be recorded as they occur. Abbreviated. Importance of including references. May be revised or edited for an audience.
To explore and maintain relationships with others	Letters, cards Questionnaires Interviews E-mail, fax, and so on	Audience often specific. May vary in formality – often demand different conventions. Inappropriate layout may confuse the message.
To predict and hypothesize	Questions, notes Opinion column Interviews Points for an argument	Personal. Often need to be recorded as they occur. Organization – may need cutting and pasting.
To make comparisons	Charts, graphs, diagrams Notes, descriptions Reviews	Often form part of a larger text for an audience. Layout all-important. Need to be clear, neatly presented.
To command or direct	Instructions, recipes Stage directions Rules – contracts	Audience often specific. May vary in formality – often demand different conventions or precise language. Inappropriate layout may confuse the message.
To amuse or entertain	Jokes, riddles, puzzles Scripts for drama Stories and poems Personal anecdotes	May be personal or for an audience. Audience may be specific. Layout and entertainment value may be more important than neatness.

A
- Autobiography
- Letter
- Pamphlet
- Story
- Notes
- Poem
- Diary
- Play
- News
- Conversation

B
- Directions
- Prayer
- Song
- List
- Schedule
- Biography
- Riddle
- Script
- Label
- Report
- Dictionary

C
- Bar chart
- Advertisement
- Notice
- Book Review
- Poster
- Quiz
- Program
- Flow chart
- Book cover
- Instructions

D
- Application form
- Menu
- Map
- Cartoon
- Crossword
- Game
- Diagram
- Recipe

Appendix 3: Three ways to plan a story

1. A Story Tree

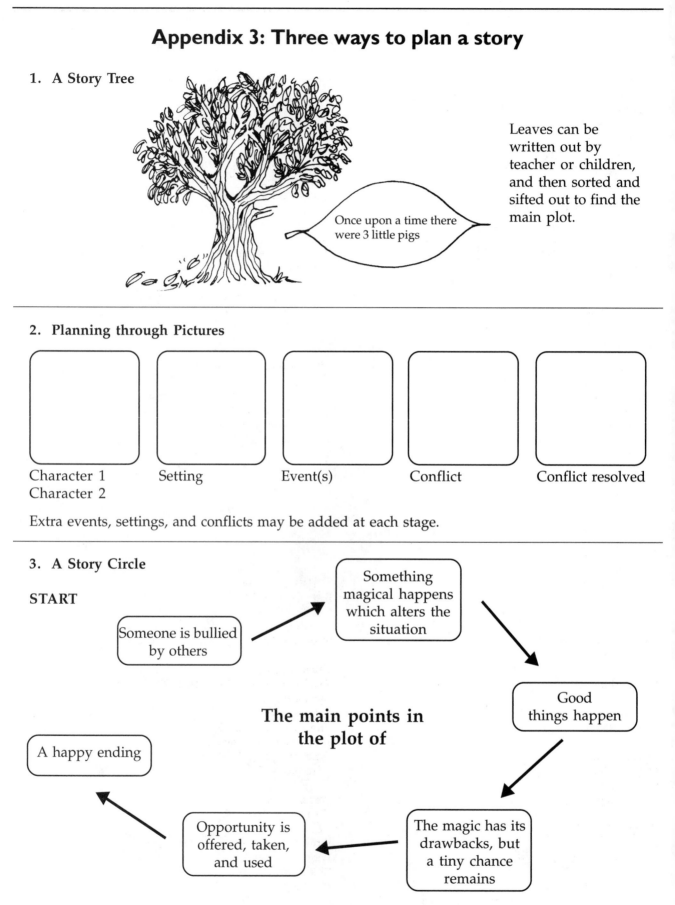

Once upon a time there were 3 little pigs

Leaves can be written out by teacher or children, and then sorted and sifted out to find the main plot.

2. Planning through Pictures

Character 1 Character 2	Setting	Event(s)	Conflict	Conflict resolved

Extra events, settings, and conflicts may be added at each stage.

3. A Story Circle

START

Someone is bullied by others

Something magical happens which alters the situation

Good things happen

The main points in the plot of

A happy ending

Opportunity is offered, taken, and used

The magic has its drawbacks, but a tiny chance remains

Each stage may be altered or expanded to create a new or "parallel" plot.

INDEX